The Book of Norman

by
Steven Kramer

Copyright 2022
Fold In
Steven Kramer

Published by Spare Pyre Productions

Cover Design by Krimson Kat Studios

ISBN: 978-1-957103-00-6
Hardcover

Dedication

Since I lack the skill set and possibly the
grandchildren and their grandchildren necessary
for verbal transmission of memory, this is my
imperfect way of sharing Norm's legacy and these
new, familiar, transitive canyons of loss.

Rest in peace Normy.
Save us seats, your army
will array one day.

The Book of Norman

Contents

Introduction

This tortured, twisting tale which will take you my friends, my gentle readers, from the wilds of Long Island, through the never fabulous Newark, New Jersey airport and to the truly wild rainforests of Vancouver Island began via e-mail when CAF informed me, "Going forward a third party building scientist will inspect each claim, determine causation and a fair path forward for all involved parties. His name is Norm Slavik and he will be contacting you shortly."

He did and ten years later. Et voila! a book of poetry for your reading pleasure.

O, I dig your skepticism babies. I mean how can a book of poetry about a building scientist, product claims and rotting wood be of any real interest to anyone beyond the building science community and perhaps those who love them? And you know even the loved ones might not actually be interested either.

And you are correct of course and for you, the wide, wide audience of the world I am working on a pulp novel about murder and small town intrigue that might be more your speed, so by all means leave this book on the shelves and wait for the launch of Murder on Fine June Morning or some other thing because I really suck at titles, maybe the editor will come up with something better. And yes, I know I just violated the first rule of writing by telling a whole swath of people to NOT read what I have written, but meh, I have bigger things to worry about, like my creaking back, trick knee and climate change.

And for you building scientists and perhaps the people who love them our tortured, twisting tale shall commence forthwith.

Part One:

Fishing the days away

Chapter 1

The first meeting…

It became immediately apparent after the first 15 minutes on the first claim I visited with Norm Slavik back in 2005 on the Main Road just west of Southold on the North Fork of Long Island that:

1. Norm possessed an innate ability to disarm very angry people who were looking at the prospect of having to undertake some very expensive repairs on their dream home that they had just recently spent wads and wads of cash to build. Very angry people with the resources available to hire very capable attorneys.

2. Norm could walk the barely visible line between informing people why they were having issues with the materials on their house without making it appear that the real culprit was the builder they had paid too much money to build their dream house and could not be bothered to use best building practices to build their very expensive dream house,

3. Norm knew building science back to front, sideways, in the rear-view mirror and he had way cool inspection gadgets like IR cameras and titanium head hammers,

4. What had been painful, problematic and damaging to all involved parties was now in the hands of someone capable of collecting data, explicating, proposing and resolving the problem at hand.

And with these realizations, the weight of seven Earths fell from my shoulders and I shall be stoned to death for saying so, but I like this little slice of alliterative, blasphemous, overstated magic: Norm of Nazareth!

Chapter 2

First trip, October 2007

1.
Norm had asked if I would like to attend
in 2006, but I politely declined as I did
almost every work related invitation (dinners,
plant tours, launch events, conferences, lunches) in
those days (I mean who wants to hang with a bunch
of *lumber* dudes on MY time?) and then
Norm sent me a few photos from the trip,
the hale and hearty army to a man smiling,
arrayed on the deck of the Quadra Island rental,
back dropped by the Discovery Passage, sun blazing,
settling behind the Island Range and I thought
if not now likely never. Needlessly indicated:
Norm's invitation in 2007 was not declined.

2.
The short flight from YVR to Campbell
River tracks the east coast of Vancouver
Island. The green scenery is hazed with
drifting clouds. The Island Range cradles
the late afternoon sun. Out of the right
window, the fjords of the mainland. Jesus,
why would anyone ever leave this place?

3.
After successfully negotiating the taxi cab
ride from the airport, our newly minted PFC in
the hale and hearty army has failed to properly
follow orders and mistakenly ended up at the
Discovery Inn watching Joba Chamberlain
get attacked by an improbably persistent swarm of
midges during the ALDS in Cleveland, downing
ice cold Kokanees, Glacier Fresh Beer, waiting
for his commanding officer and the rest of the army
until CdJ and DB arrive. Kramer? Yes sir! You're
in the wrong place. Sorry about that. Come
with us, we're late for the ferry to Quadra.

4.
Despite imbibing several sedative brews, jet lag
and an all night constant, pouring rain amplified by
the roof of the rented barracks keep our humble PFC
awake all night. He thinks there is no way we can fish in
this. This is his first of many, repetitious, incorrect estimations
and assumptions about the mountains, rainforests and weather of
coastal British Columbia. Poor boy. He thinks he actually knows
things.

5.
The hale and hearty army, equally divided among three boats (Hunter
boat, Norm's boat, The New Zealand boat) is indeed fishing the next
day. The newly minted PFC from back east (still waiting for his sea
legs to arrive via slow boat/Pony Express/parcel post/bus from
Albuquerque) gets
to take first turn at the rod and try his luck at landing silver.

6.
The heavy trolling tackle overwhelms the first FISH ON! The
green PFC thinks several times he has lost the fish, but
Curtis says keep reeling it's on there and soon enough
there's silver in the boat. It's a small hatchery coho (clipped
adipose fin) We get to keep this one after the flash of requisite
bloody dispatching violence (reader discretion is advised)

WHACK! (the small ones only need one WHACK!)

And the photos of course. Jesus, smile Kramer! When you get
home, put that one on the grill. Any other preparation would be
a sin. Sir, yes sir!

7.
With varying result which we shall get to eventually this
will become a yearly rite, like the first robins on the lawn jigging
for worms when the frost starts to leave the ground or the swamp
maple along the fence line shading red in mid-August weeks
before the others all follow suit. A rite to mark the passage of
the year, the quickly approaching winter replete with blood
sacrifice, kneeling at altars and fine beverage alcohol.

All Hail!

Chapter 3

Getting there…

By necessity and otherwise, Norm
never consecutively scheduled the exact
same route or means of transport into Cam River:

1.
Year one, was the standard route and means your
local travel agent would schedule for you: Air Canada flight
from JFK into YVR, the only non-stop direct
flight from NYC, arriving in Vancouver at 11AM
local time, this was 2007 before the housing bubble
burst and all of the interconnected wagers dissembled
to dust and the economy collapsed so Norm flew me
out first class with a window seat. The flight
pattern took us directly over Niagara Falls which
was clearly visible from 30,000 feet and that luxury
and beauty was beyond sufficient, but while hiking
to catch my regional flight to Campbell River at the very
distal end of the domestic flight terminal I caught
sight of the North Shore Mountains not miles distant, but
so close beyond the glass I figured (incorrectly
for certain) that I could walk there in about four
steps and I thought   Geezus why would anyone
                          leave this place?

2.
There were ferry rides,
Horseshoe Bay to Departure Bay
Tsawwassen to Duke Point
Duke Point to Tsawwassen

We are lucky to have ferries back home on Long Island and they
are always (except in high seas after a late night in Boston) a
fun and interesting means of transit and having a beer
on a ferry is a singular pleasure, but the BC
boats are not boats really, but ambulatory cities moving
people and freight between the mainland and
Vancouver Island.

3.
One year Norm had me take a float plane from
the YVR float plane terminal into Nanaimo.

Somewhere, I think in the old Motorola flip phone that we used until
December of last year (so cute, so behind the times) there is a photo of an
icy Kokanee, Glacier Fresh Beer, and a pile of salt and pepper ribs
backstopped by a beautiful view of Nanaimo harbor.

Isn't technology great?

4.
The best part of the ferry and float planes was the resultant
ride up Highway 19 to Campbell River when Norm, myself,
RM and or DB would shoot the shit, catch up, steel
ourselves for the approaching war or taunt a once
hale and hearty soldier who did not make the trip that year.

Often while shooting the shit, catching up, steeling
for the approaching war and taunting absent soldiers Norm
would also be engaged in an on off on off dialogue via his
hands free cellular telephone device trading details, action items,
brinkmanship maneuvers on his latest projects:
auditing the 2006 Softwood Lumber Agreement, the
Ted Leroy Trucking bankruptcy, due diligence
efforts to support a play for the old Elk Falls pulp
mill outside Campbell River, brokering the sale
of the West Fraser Skeena mill in Terrace, resolving
a convoluted product claim replete with very unhappy
lawsuit ready property owners, expediting the testing results
for biomass work being conducted on behalf
of a German consortium or untangling the familial
post-War real estate mess back in Latvia.

5.
Getting there:
half the battle
half the fun and
if you were not
too dazzled by, too
focused on the
over the top

you must be kidding me
why would anyone ever
leave this place?
beauty of Vancouver
Island playing past
your window
a graduate level class
in entrepreneurship
was being offered
free of charge.

Chapter 4

Dana

One of Norm's closest friends and also his chiropractor.

A funny, just considered thought: my advice
to sciatica sufferers is to keep your friends
close and your chiropractor closer.

Please insert rim shot here gentle reader.

An ever smiling, good natured dude,
loving husband and father, Dana
always greeted the Yank
contingent of our hale and hearty
army, "My American friends!"

I am still trying to figure
out what Dana did to whom
whereby the offended party
saw fit to invoke a peasant
curse involving
Dana and his interactions
with Curtis'
fishing tackle.

So much broken
equipment, it had
to be a curse.

Right?

Chapter 5

Pacific white sided dolphins...

Frequent and never refused cetacean hitchhikers, riding the Grady's
bow wave, now skiing the wake between powerful airborne
leaps offering free entertaining diversion and numerous photographic
opportunities (I hear they call these photo-ops) as we make
the long run to The Wall, Plumper or Deepwater for another
day trolling for silver.

But your gathered, streaking, leaping multitude (tens? hundreds?
thousands?) off the Chatham Point light heading south into
The Passage from Johnstone Strait turned an unproductive
Chum season into a singular life event.

I hereby invoke the indigenous magic of the temperate coastal rain
forest or perhaps Western deific intercession not pedestrian,
mathematic coincidence to explain this.

Chapter 6

You will never be ready…

Trust me.

You will never be ready.

You will be hunched against the wind and a
cold constant October drizzle, your
thumbs hooked into the elastic
suspenders of your deep green rain gear OR
you will be feline stretched near napping in
the sun sponging its gloried restorative rays OR
you will be in the middle of a meaning
of Life philosophical moment, the glowing green, sun,
clouds, mountains and waters of British Columbia are especially
inspirational in regards to philosophical meaning
of Life moments OR
watching anything, but the three taut lines behind
the boat, the bald eagle high on the bluff, the lone bull sea lion
picking his way through the fishing fleet,
the twisting dance of clouds as they descend from
Menzies into Discovery Passage, now
gathering into a darkening threat OR
cracking Spitz, eating Pringles or giant chocolate chip
cookies, gnawing on Nanaimo bars or the lunch
Norm ordered from the kitchen at Painter's Lodge the night
before and with unerring certainty picked up right after
we ate breakfast in Legends Dining Room OR
you could be engaged in a gentlemanly, pointed
exchange regarding the familial heritage,
lack of facility in Life or angling ability or penchant for cross
dressing with another member of the hale
and hearty crew OR
nursing a hangover the roughly size and
geographic complexity of Yellowstone National Park OR
getting a head start on tomorrow's hangover, drinking
coffee spritzed with Bailey's Irish Cream, having a
bracing slug from the split of The Glenlivet, beer number
fourteen, one more cocktail before rods up OR

you could be caught (children and those easily
offended please cover your ears) literally with your dick
in hand releasing the coffee, Bailey's, Scotch and beer
back to the Earth OR
on a very slow day, arcing a bear banger over
the bow of the boat holding the other members
of the hale and hearty army BAM,
the list of distractions is likely endless…until

WHAM!

Someone (most usually Curtis or Gene) yells
FISH ON!

And from beneath whatever distraction was holding
sway you launch yourself toward the offending, jerking
rod, grab it (quickly but carefully) from its holder (especially
tricky on the outrigger set off port, you do not want to send a rod to
the depths of the fjord trailing migratory silver) and from
the wheelhouse Curtis is admonishing
reel, reel, reel,
reel, reel, reel,
pop the clip
pop the clip
so you rear and
pop, pop, pop
to free the line from the downrigger and
you finally feel some idea what you might
have hooked into and if you play your line
right and with Curtis' or Gino's deft
net skills manage to boat the beast and it's
not a fancy fish (Drucker) you have one for
the box, but first a photo, Geezus smile Kramer, tilt
the fish back to catch the sun, hold the head
toward me and then a taunt over the two way,
six in the boat, six in the boat we're
killing it today and a crackling the day's not over
boys or I heard your Mom kills it retort and the ten minutes
of action is replaced by a return to the distracting
revelry until again summoned:

FISH ON!

Trust me.

You will never be ready.

Chapter 7

Coho salmon…

Fancy fish (Drucker) in The Passage become red rockets in the rivers
struggling toward sex and doom. They are aggressive when hitting
our spinners (they're pissed off at our silly
intrusion, they do not feed once in their natal rivers,) now
wild with arcing, shaking acrobatic leaps when we
somehow manage (from the beneath the staggering
gauzy haze of hangover) to properly set the hook.

Do not worry big fella, release is imminent
once someone snaps a well-focused photo.

Meanwhile in The Passage, hatchery
Cohos (clipped adipose fin) fresh, sleek, silver
will end up on the grill.

Sorry dude, but you are delicious and unlike
your wild brothers you are not
protected by Fisheries and Oceans Canada.

Chapter 8

Chum salmon...

Our primary October ocean quarry, I hear tell
the commercial men sell your kind at five
cents a pound for pet food. A sad end for
a burly fighter that can send a stout man
ass over electric kettle into the mighty, mighty Campbell.

I prefer a more fitting tribute:
pepper smoked by High Tide Seafood in Cam River,
jerked into marvelous sweet/savory Indian Candy or
baked simply and then flaked into Thai scented fish cakes.

Pet food my ass!

I hereby rename you Keta salmon and will
initiate a proper public relations campaign to
transmogrify you into the Canadian
version of Chilean sea bass!

Chapter 9

Forestry poem…

Until you no longer wipe
your ass with toilet paper or
clean up the baby's or the dog's
or your mess with a paper towel.

Until you no longer build or
live in houses constructed of
lumber or sit on chairs, couches
and recliners constructed from
wood entirely or in part.

Until the poets cease
polluting ream upon ream of
clean white paper, you all
must stop complaining
about forest clear cuts.

While I agree it appears a destroyed
moonscape after the saws,
feller bunchers, skidders,
yarders, processors, trucks
and the men wielding them have
had their way with the land, but
what the spinning photographs,
articles and documentaries fail
to show is the cleared, piled slash
burning to quickly return nutrients
to the soil and the tree for tree,
specie for specie re-planting that
occurs once the land is
cleared and here is the truth they
will never reveal because it
ruins their tale and you would
never know until you saw the hills
and mountains and islands of BC with
its forests in multiple stages of
maturity, it all grows back.

Sure, not in 5 years, but in forty,
fifty or ninety years so that the
men with the saws, feller
bunchers, skidders,
yarders, processors and trucks can
return and harvest the trees so
your grandchildren and their
grandchildren can build
houses, sit on chairs, clean
up the floor beneath the baby and
her bowl of spaghetti in marinara, pollute
pure white paper with poetry and wipe their asses.

Chapter 10

David

I discovered a specific glee when David
taunted our hale and hearty army
with candied squid jerky and thousand
year old eggs and turned gruff, grown
men debating lumber and whiskey into
a gaggle of giggling school kids:
I ain't eating that.
You eat it.
Your Mom eats it.
No not me, you.
Ewww! Smells like a thousand-year-old fart.

Yet the grown man part reasserts when it comes to a wager, a hundred
bucks to the first man to eat one of those stinking eggs.

The wager goes uncollected.

Me? I wager that house still holds the faint
odor of a thousand-year-old fart and the owners
cannot seem to find out
why.

In my sulfurous haze, I almost forgot to mention
that David's snoring is the stuff of legend, local
children still sing songs about the monster
asleep on Quadra Island:

From up north by Brown's Bay
south over Courtenay way,
you can hear him snoring
noon, night or morning,
the monster of Quadra Island.

Chapter 11

The night at Dolphin's Resort…

We had enjoyed an excellent if occasionally very
raucous meal and after dinner digestives at the
Anglers' Dining Room (where better for we fishers
of fish to seek repast?) and I never thought much
about it until the hale and hearty army never made a return
engagement to said establishment even
though the food was a cut above most other
places in and around Campbell River, but now
reviewing the Dolphin's Resort website
Fine Dining with Casual Flair…check
Innovative Italian inspired seafood menu
reflecting the seasonal bounty of both
Campbell River and Vancouver Island…check
Gourmet cuisine…check
Served in an intimate oceanfront setting…oh…
I see why never made a return
engagement at said establishment even
though the food was a cut above most other
places around Campbell River. An intimate
oceanfront setting is no place for a hale and hearty
army, no matter the size and I am also understanding
the slightly askew looks and quiet flashing anger of
the other dinner guests they disguised so readily
with wide grins.

A good general must know best where to
bivouac his troops and there were for all
parties more suitable fields for our tents.

Chapter 12

The forays…

Before the hale and hearty army arrived in its
multitudes and arrayed finery, Norm and I had to foray, forage
and skirmish into the wilds of Campbell River to secure supplies:

First groceries for the cabins and boat snacks/accoutrements from
the bustling and perilous aisles of Save-On at rush hour:

Boursin cheese	Pringles
smoked gouda	Spitz
crackers	ginger ale
salumi	orange juice
gluten free pepperettes	
kilo of thinly sliced deli	
roast beef	
apples (really Norm?)	

After stashing our haul of foodstuffs, we crossed the vast, dangerous,
unknown, possible catastrophe our constant companion, parking lot for adult
refreshments from BC Liquor a 2-4 of Kokanee, Glacier
Fresh beer, a couple sixers of Strongbow, a few bottles of J Lohr
cab sauv and a bottle of chardonnay just in case, 2 splits
of The Glenlivet, 2 splits of Bailey's Irish Cream, one bottle
Havana Club dark rum, one bottle brand irrelevant vodka,

Finally on the return leg to the cabins we would obtain the requisite
paperwork from Fisheries and Oceans Canada at River Sportsmen
between the bridges, saltwater licenses for most, fresh water for the few
accepting the yoke of river fishing, both for those competing in
the hale and hearty army's version of the Ironman triathlon:
river fishing,
ocean fishing and
consumption of the adult
refreshment stash meant
for twenty men, not eight, in
addition to myriad beverages
consumed on the boats, with passable
meat appetizers, over dinner, after

dinner, at 2AM and right
before bed.

Prayer: Dearest liver, halest and heartiest of all
organs, I hope some day you will forgive
me, until then put on your helmet son
it is going to get ugly down there.

Chapter 13

Steller sea lions…

1.
Clustered big, brown and ponderous on the shore
above Ripple Rock, taking a bit of restorative sun between
frigid swim and the cold, drizzling rain of five minutes ago.

O sweet, changeable weather of coastal British Columbia!

It is that…or there are Orca in the channel and the sun drenched
rocks are more about self preservation than warm soothing nap.

In either case, say cheese everyone. We're taking photos, well
focused and otherwise.

2.
Everyone watches warily, a bull lion is moving
gracefully, diving, surfacing with a watery snort, slowly
picking his way through the fishing fleet.

All are worried that he will scare the fish.
A reasonable concern that, but I am
transfixed, jealous the way water transforms
his ponderous, brown bulk of rocky shore into
a fluid, fast, deadly hunter.

I need to get me some of that.
The transformation from ponderous
bulk into graceful fluidity thing not
the deadly hunter gig.

Chapter 14

The night Norm got a wild hair across his arse...

> Let's take the air and walk
> to the Quinsam boys.

It was a wondrous, cool night, I was
a new recruit to the hale and hearty army
and Norm had haunted the streets of
Cam River since the 70s, so I agreed and we
set out across the lot in the general
direction of the Quinsam Hotel, a singular
shall we say distinctive night spot in Cam River.

Like kids, we kicked along a squished
pop can for the first few blocks as
the cool night air cleared some of the
boozy haze from our heads.

I am not sure when exactly it kicked
in, but eventually, also like a kid, I had
to say something
hey Norm it's not much farther is it?

> Not too far, no.

Onward we trudged, our foray
approaching the point of ceaseless
endeavour when the Quinsam Hotel,
singular distinctive night spot of Cam River,
came into view at last. As we reached for
the door, I said to Norm, so maybe we
don't want to do that again.

> It was a bit further than I

projected.

Liquor does strange things to
distance, time and memory gentle reader, so
in the interest of fact based poetry and
real life reportage, I just punched our

route into Mapquest (Ain't technology great?) which revealed we had walked roughly 4 and ½ miles for a beer.

There's a television commercial or marketing slogan in
there somewhere.

Chapter 15

Cees

Norm's protégé, mock nemesis and verbal fencing foil.

For propriety's sake I shall not repeat their
gentlemanly, pointed exchanges regarding
each other's national heritage, lack
of facility in Life or
penchant for cross
dressing, suffice it to say, said
exchanges were (damn! how
do I say this diplomatically…vocabulary
do not fail me now…ah yes…) pungent.

O and Cees? This stolen, transmogrified lyric loops
through my thoughts: We remember you well in the
Quinsam Hotel.

Yes indeed we do.

Chapter 16

I always considered Norm a Canadian in good standing…

Temperate in mood, prone to kind diplomacy in difficult
times, a cool head inclined toward reason when things
really and actually turned to utter shit, so I was shocked
the first time Norm said   Hey, let's grab a Starbucks.

I countered   But, there's a Timmie's right across
                                            the street. Let's grab a double
                                            double.

                                            I can't drink that crap.

Treason!
Blasphemy!

Chapter 17

Bald eagle…

Are ubiquitous in coastal BC, like the red
tailed hawks perched in small skeletal elms silently scanning the freshly mown
medians and shoulders of the New York
State Thruway back home, yet if you come
to believe raptored majesty (bald, red tailed or
other) as somehow commonplace or boring, I
hereby revoke your human card.

Chapter 18

I fall into the mighty, mighty Campbell…twice…

1.
I am fly fishing for the first time in any
river anywhere, our hale and hearty army
working (as much as a crew of neophyte fly
fisherman can work) a prime honey hole below
the hydro-electric dam on the Campbell River, the mighty
mighty Campbell, when a fish rose and slammed
my drifting pink fly.

I reared to set the hook (successfully I must
add,) but kept going back, back, back until I
reached and then very quickly exceeded gravitational
equilibrium, the tipping point between standing/reclining and fell
ass backward into the mighty, mighty Campbell.

Despite the surprise of falling ass backward into rushing
icy water, I manage to maintain a cogent thought
train (I am quite good at falling) so in my
mind I keep repeating:
keep the tip up,
keep the tip up,
keep the tip up,
while with Curtis' assistance I regain a proper
standing position such that I am able to fight, land and after
photos, release a sizable Chum salmon fresh,
silver, newly arrived in the river.

2.
It has been a disappointing day on the mighty, mighty
Campbell, a cold unrelenting rain has kept the fish away
from our flies and last night encroached well into this morning so
our hale and hearty army while ambulatory are suffering
quietly beneath the solitary hammer of terrible hangovers.

Even Norm who knows, respects and rarely exceeds
the limits of bad behaviour did not excuse himself

from our 2AM erudite exchanges on environmental
politics, philosophy or overindulgence in Scotch whiskey.

Even Norm who usually maintains a running
dialogue of digs, barbs and insults with Curtis regarding
the others' many and varied shortcomings is suffering
quietly beneath the solitary hammer of a terrible hangover.

So Curtis steers the raft toward shore just below the bridges and tries
one more time to unsuccessfully bait Norm, "One more try before
we head in you useless, hungover S.O.Bs."

In violation of pontoon dogma (both feet over the side at the same time son)
I
try to step out of the raft which now free of my substantial burden pops
high in the water, but shit! my left foot is stuck and damn it I am again
meeting then very quickly exceeding gravitational
equilibrium, the tipping point between standing/reclining, but
this time before I can go fully into the water Norm and Curtis grab
hold and try to keep me upright, but after a few seconds of
struggle trying to free my left foot I tell them, "Just let me go," and for
the second time in two years, I have fallen into the mighty, mighty Campbell.

I scramble to standing, but this time my water resistant wind
breaker has proven unequal to the task such that it appears
the term water resistant came from Jack in Marketing not
from science or practice and although I can not really say
so (there's no whining on the mighty, mighty Campbell) I am soaked
well and through and will soon be quite cold.

3.
I will allow that two spills into the mighty, mighty Campbell may
lead one to surmise that I am a damned klutz. If you must.

I see my spills into the mighty, mighty Campbell as
payment, homage, a little slice of humor for the god(s) of the river
in exchange for allowing me:

to land a sizable Chum salmon still fresh, silver, newly
arrived to the river,

to fight and with Curtis' assistance land a 40 pound (sorry 20
kilogram) Chinook salmon later that same day,

to watch the steam rising from my soaked water resistant wind
breaker, the re-conquering sun backlighting a bald eagle perched in
a hemlock above Raven Park, floating with Norm and Curtis beneath
the ebbing hammer of hangover, cold as hell, perfect, immortal.

In exchange for these memories I would fall
into the mighty, mighty Campbell forty times.

Chapter 19

The fuck poem…

Again your mind in the gutter gentle, salacious
reader? Really? You should look into a hobby.

What I really wanted to convey is the following:
after reading a poem contained in this collection
Curtis relayed the following feedback

> I like the poem Kramer,
> but you are missing a few
> fucks.

Truer words are rarely spoken, so here gentle
gutter minded reader are a few fucks. Please
insert them into the conversational portions (or
wherever the fuck you want, what the fuck) of these
poems as you see fit:

fuck (ellipse)
FUCK (exclamation point)
Fuck (comma)
f (carriage return)
u (carriage return)
c (carriage return)
k (carriage return)
fucken, fucken, fuckety, fuck, fuck
fucking
blowjob
(Dr. Les requested that I include one also in the name
of accuracy)
F (period) U (period) C (period) K (period)
Fuck (period.)

If you use these up, please contact my
attorney, we will send more.

The most disappointing Fuck Poem you have
ever read is now over gentle, filthy reader.

Chapter 20

Chinook salmon…

Large, prized, elusive, was that you out by
The Wall seized by seal and lost for all time?

It is possible.

I know it was you on the mighty, mighty Campbell (I have
an un-doctored, well focused photo as proof) that
we (Curtis and myself) landed you after a lengthy, line
peeling, bruised knuckle battle with your
40 pound (sorry 20 kilogram) immensity and the swift
line shearing current.

That was my first time fly fishing any river
anywhere and I thought catching 40 pound
(sorry 20 kilogram) Chinooks was standard
happenstance, not a singular life event.

Silly boy, have an apple from
the interspeciel dumb tree.

Chapter 21

Confession…

That first beautiful
hatchery Coho,
cleaned, filleted,
vacuum sealed and
shipped three thousand
miles east at goodly
expense
ended up not
on the grill, but
breaded and pan
fried in butter Polish style.

Forgive me,
if you
can Norm.

Chapter 22

Rigas melnais Balzams

The unofficial drink of the
homeland, Latvija,
a subtle, bitter haze for
the new initiates,
now with 29 herbs and spices,
inky ball sweat of
demons more
precisely.

They say it's a great
cure for colds.

Sure. Why not?

Chapter 23

A gentlemanly exchange regarding the angling skill level of our hale and hearty crew…

Let us start with a simple mathematical ratio exercise based on failing memory and estimate: For every fish our hale and hearty crew landed on ocean and in river, I posit that at least three swam free after nudging our spinners, hoochies or anchovies taunting strikes that an angler with any degree of skill above none would have responded with a properly set hook and after a brief, beautiful battle, would have landed their shimmering silver quarry. Smiling photos for everyone!

Despite our horrible catch ratio, Curtis (our expert guide to the endless fresh, salt and brackish waters of Vancouver Island whose own skill set on said waters so exceeded the aforementioned lack of ability of our hale and hearty crew to land fish to the point where we should bow and express our utter lack of worth,)

with steeled, smiling, Canadian patience, good cheer and gentlemanly reassurance would offer,

Never mind. We'll get the next one boys.

Except if Norm were the guilty party whereupon Curtis would offer with steeled, smiling, Canadian patience and good cheer,

Geez Normy, you fucking missed that one eh? You know it's hard enough putting you guys on fish, if you're not going to bother

hooking them, we might as well
head home.

On slow days with taunting strikes, even
gentle nudges few and far
between Norm would return serve,

Geezus Christ Curtis where are the
fucking fish? A GOOD guide
would know where to go. It seems
I might have overestimated your
ability. Look! That boat over there
is landing one now. Maybe I will
book them next year."

A never invoked threat
for comedic effect only.

Thank the indigenous gods of these
endless fresh, salt and brackish
waters of Vancouver Island.

Chapter 24

Marek…

The voluble
Zubrowka swilling
polymer chemist was the only
member of the hale and hearty army
who was wholly and entirely
unaffected by the beautiful, myriad mind
diversions of fishing in coastal BC, instead
he repeatedly
pop, pop, popped the clip,
reel, reel, reeled even when
the line was disturbed not by
fleet silver, but by kelp, by
random flotsam, by
merest floating twig.

Each popped clip and retrieved empty
line required Curtis, in equal measure, but
with exceedingly more effort, to reset the popped
rig, two rigs when Marek saw
fit to pop the outrigger.

Marek elicited the only flash of true
anger I saw from Curtis, in seven
years, "OK Marek, from now
on, no more reeling unless I say
FISH ON!"

Chapter 25

The forests of coastal British Columbia…

Are alive.
Of course they are. There are millions of trees out there.
I do not mean it like that, more precisely
I mean IT is alive, a giant singular being
its millions upon millions of trees mere
cells in a greater whole. Listen dude, you
can hear it breathing and look the way it
cracks a glowing green smile after the rains
abate and the sun steals in, a sneak thief.

Too much I think.

                                        A sound hypothesis
                                        which we could prove
                                        readily with science.

                        Hey will one of you two
                        philosophy students
                        grab the outrigger and land
                        the damned fish that's biting?

                        FISH ON!

You will never be ready.

Chapter 26

Sometimes, I just do not get it…

And I become a bit of a nuisance like when I
injected business into the calling forth of the hale
and hearty army, Hey Norm, since we are in the cradle
of the North American forest industry, would it not be
beneficial if we took the opportunity to conduct some
educational efforts around these trips? Ever the
accommodating Canadian, Norm likely said something
akin to   Absolutely Steve. I agree,
                                                       let's do it.
while in the back of his mind he more likely said I like Steve, I think he's a
nice guy, but he just does not get it.

The effort started modestly that first year, before catching
the flight to Vancouver, we headed North of Campbell River
and checked out a clear cut just off Highway 19. Somewhere
likely in the old flip phone we used until last December, there
are photos of a steep hillside awaiting reclamation by
fire and seedling. We took a quick spin through a dry land
sort on the way back into town. The big Cat log loaders
and their immense grapples dormant for the weekend. No
photos, sorry. Think piles of logs and big yellow machines.

The following year, Norm brought Doctor Les aboard
to give a seminar on everything you ever wanted to
know about trees, but did not even know what questions
to ask. The only business seminar I've been party to where we
attendees drank before, *during* and after the presentation. It was…
spirited and highly informative. Doctor Les may be the only
man in this hemisphere, perhaps the world who can transform
forestry science and dendrochronology into the most interesting
subjects ever, more Merlin than Mendel.

One year, before hitting the ferries for The Island we
took a day trip to Forintek at the University of British Columbia to discuss
emerging markets for coastal forest products with the scientists and
researchers there which the villainous VP of acquisitions, overseas trade and

riverboat casinos disrespectfully dominated to our shock, awe and later deep amusement.

There was a stop at an Island custom cut mill operation that
I could not attend because we missed the ferry and ended
up eating lunch in the Village of Horseshoe Bay, more on
that later.

We did a field trip to several construction sites in and around Campbell River to demonstrate best building practices and how best to address water infiltration into building envelopes all beneath the heavy hammer of particularly wicked hangovers.

I am probably boring you to tears eh gentle reader with these wooden recollections?

I already told you, sometimes I just do not get it and become
a bit of a nuisance. There again, you might learn something
if you stand next to me. Like how to bore people with
recollections about forestry and science.

Hey…I never said I was Dr. Les.

Chapter 27

Black tailed deer: Catching the 5AM ferry in Nanaimo…

As if by magic or deific intercession (I again refuse
to believe in the boring math of coincidence) I
woke suddenly to familiar
reflective blue eyes in the middle
of the road and calmly said:

Hey Norm, wake up. There's a fucking
deer in the middle of the road.

                                            Oh yeah.
                                            Thanks.

No problem.

With a similar lack of fanfare or concern
that Norm appeared to be dozing
at the wheel I went
quietly back to sleep.

Like I said FUCKING magic

Chapter 28

Saviour...

After a catastrophe of misinterpretation,
misunderstanding, failed
extrapolation and finger pointing,
when every one else was
an echo chamber returning useless anger
and acid disbelief, you (acknowledging
your own useless anger and acid
disbelief) delineated a plan of fact and algebra:
ask one
if one is answered in the affirmative,
then state two
if two then
state three
if three then
four.

Alternately, if one is answered in
the negative then fuck 'em. It's time to
move on.

Life is too short to
suffer the tyranny
of lies.

Chapter 29

Harbor seals…

Are the bane of fishing fleets the world over, in
British Columbia silent swift salmon thieves.

The rod I hold is bent hard over, clearly I am
making zero progress in bringing the fish boat
ward so Curtis speculates, "I think we might have hooked
a Chinook there big fella." Just then line begins
to peel from the reel by noisy yards (sorry
meters, my Canadian friends,) and Curtis
dejectedly cuts the line, "Fucking seal. Dammit!"

But no one can resist the stupid cute
one eyed survivor of a boat
propeller accident,
haunting the marina,
carting off salmon heads
and recycling the
sweet, sweet entrails.

Circle of Life baby!

A water's edge cycloptic trash man without
the gruff persona and cheap cigar.

Chapter 30

Poem for Moxie's of Campbell River…

The evening's battle often began with skirmishing at Moxie's:

Reason 1

It was next door to the marina and on occasion Curtis and Norm
might forego the formality of having the entire army offload the boats
and take photos of the day's catch spiffily arranged on the dock and we would
hop off at the fuel pier, amble up the gangplank and into the bar our
clothes, hands, toques and boots fresh with the pungent remnants of the day's
fishing.

I think most of us washed our hands and ran a damp paper towel over our
wind wild hair before proceeding toward the bar. I think.

Reason 2

There was a large bar so that the hale and hearty army could fully
array its handsome multitude and uniformed finery. See above.

Reason 3

They made Frozen Bellinis, Norm's favorite drink.

Reason 4

The staff without easily recollected exception was always very accommodating
allowing members of the hale and hearty army wide liberty for instance:

Running a demonstration on how to make a real Tom Collins god dammit,
not that
crap with the fucking sour mix Geezus does anyone know how to tend
bar anymore? You will need a couple of whole lemons and some simple
syrup! No simple syrup? Fucking hell. Two packets of sugar then. Christ
on the cross! What is the world coming to?

Forgiving instances where in their absence one of our number may have slipped
behind the bar and reinforced our beverages, not for the sake of free, but because
our glasses were nearly empty and our never abundant patience had officially run out,

engaging in conversation with a bunch of wind and sun fried dudes whose
clothes, hands, toques and boots were fresh with the pungent remnants of the day's
fishing, likely did not shower that morning and whose general appearance
approached that of an arrayed line of sun and wind cured Charles Manson
stand ins.

Reason 5

Someone must sing the praises of the thorough and very
attentive gay bartender. Craig?

Reason 6

Passably decent meat appetizers. In all honesty, that is a low
bar of achievement, after a long day on the water we would
have eaten microwaved, gluten free fish sticks with ketchup.

Reason 7

It was the only place in Campbell River with a bar large enough that
the hale and hearty army could fully array its handsome multitude and uniformed
finery, where the staff would engage in jousting conversation with a bunch of
sun and wind cured Charles Manson stand ins without flinching, where we could order
passable meat snacks and Norm could drink his favorite frozen Bellinis.

Moxie's of Campbell River…a singular dining and drinking establishment for sure.

O right I forgot. It's a chain with 65 locations throughout Canada.

Chapter 31

Black bear...

We saw black bear once while floating an always to remain unnamed
river on The Island north of the mighty, mighty Campbell (unlike
Norm I shall not carelessly reveal Curtis' secret honey
holes even in the name of poetic exactitude) our raucous,
hale and hearty crew (redolent of hangover breath, yesterday's
whiskey spills and meat farts too numerous to count)
kicked up a black beauty from its sleeping nook on a small
islet in the river it was but a black flash
crashing into the thick riparian
underbrush really, not so much a bear
sighting really, more of a bear ass
sighting.

Then again in a cove off The Passage we sighted
one from a distance on the return leg of a run
to The Wall. The next day, like our once steadfast
now quietly vanishing postal workers, the bear was back
on its daily rounds and like excited children we floated in
silently for a closer
look.

After photos of the meandering brute, one of our
noisy number frisbeed giant oatmeal cookies onto the shore
for a wee bear snack.

No comments from the "you should not feed the wild
life" environmentalist peanut gallery please. You have
failed to note that I said we floated in
like excited children, clearly we did not know any better.

Chapter 32

The Bellini…

The frozen Bellini sat on the bar at Moxie's, melting
toward room temperature. Craig and I had ordered
the drink (a special of the house) because we thought
Norm would enjoy the frozen peach cocktail replete
with whipped cream and cherry.

But Norm preferring the dry bite of J Lohr cabernet sauvignon ignored our
offering and so it sat for the remainder of the evening, a slowly diminishing
ball of frozen drink floating in a pool of its thawed self, a ring of
condensation
spreading, soaking the paper napkin until Dr. Les seized the glass, powered
it down and scolded, "Gentlemen, you must know it iz a sin to vaste alcohol."

Chapter 33

Roosevelt Elk…

Whispering so as not to spook them
(two cows, one bull)
mid-bugling mating ritual,
"Holy shit! Look at the size of that rack!"

Curtis whispers, "He's a pretender, a
juvenile. They won't mate with
him. The mature bull is
around and will run him off
soon enough."

Later on the phone with Agnes, "I
saw three elk today and a
penultimate
cock block."

Chapter 34

The hale and hearty army also travels on its stomach…

Much like another European generalissimo of vertically challenged stature, Norm knew that his hale and hearty army also traveled on its stomach. So there were always:

Big 6AM breakfasts to grind down the sharpest
edges of hangover at the Java Shack,
Legends Dining Room, The White Spot or if late to
the water breakfast sandwiches from Tim
Horton's that never quite lived up to the
high bar of their excellent coffee and donuts, but
put something of greasy, curative substance in
angry, sour stomachs.

On the water there were snacks, Pringles,
Spitz or Curtis might share a stash of Indian candy or
smoked salmon from High Tide he had secreted in
the Grady's cabin.

Later, out came immense boxed lunches from
Java Shack or Painter's with sandwiches, giant
chocolate cookies in Saran Wrap, Nanaimo
bars and fruit. I am not really sure how the fruit
got in there. Norm's last stab at having a healthy
army perhaps? Maybe it was all about
preventing scurvy?

Fresh from the boats and before the evening's
onslaught there were preparatory skirmishes
over appetizers at Moxie's or the Tyee Pub.

Then dinner, if in a sedentary mood at
the aforementioned establishments or we
might move further afield and foray to
Royal Coachman Neighbourhood Pub,
RipTide Pub,
The Anglers Dining Room at Dolphin's Resort

or April Point Dining Room.

Once dinner and the siege of various beverage
alcohol purveyors (usually Tyee Pub,
Moxie's again, JJ's Pub, The Quinsam Hotel) reached
its necessary terminus we would repair to the well
stocked cabins for nightcaps and midnight (ahem) snacks:
Boursin cheese on crackers,
salami carefully sliced with a 2AM knife,
deli roast beef rolled into meat cigars,
gluten free pepperettes, if adventurous or
utterly hammered David's fishy/sweet
squid jerky and chips all sorts which concluded
with Norm pronouncing before hitting his rack   We're on the water by
                                                    7AM boys.
                                                    Assemble for breakfast by
                                                    6:30.

Rinse and repeat for up to five days and four
nights and you begin to understand the term
hale and hearty army O skeptical, gentle
Reader.

Chapter 35

Pink salmon…

We fished the September Pink run once.

It was productive, but honestly the Pinks lack
game and so our hale and hearty endeavor shifted
back to the late October Chum run.

It could be argued that the Pink's lack of game was
but secondary causation and instead the remnant heat of the BC
summer (it caused our hale and hearty army's mammoth
hangovers to throb into the unbearable range,) brought about
the return to cooler heads of the autumn monsoon.

Look at us: transferring our feeble failings to a humble fish.

Chapter 36

The photos…

Often times when I asked so what's up with you Norm?
Norm sent photos:

a clear cut Norm was working in an
unbelievably dense stand of hemlock,

the tricky old growth Douglas fir that had to be
dropped in the name of a right of way for a new
power line,

the vacant parcel of familial land in Latvia, recovered from the
depredations of the War and squatters that Norm sold
to the government in the name of a new highway off ramp,

the buildings of the West Fraser Skeena mill in Terrace,

photos documenting two reasons why things from
China are so damned cheap:

1. A dump truck devoid of tailgate with
an unbalanced, overweight load of large boulders, tires nearly flat, rolling
down the Interstate as if on a Sunday jaunt in the country, a
dump truck with an overweight unbalanced load of boulders
that would not have made it five feet down a North American
highway without official intervention and severe, expensive sanction,

2. A saw mill frighteningly and completely devoid of safety features, its
six foot tall, you can feel its spinning power from twenty feet, split
a careless, tripping man in sloppy halves in 1/100 of a second blade is
free to spin without the encumbrance of guards or emergency shutoffs,

kids working the pond, creek and gentle falls of the new backyard
water feature for the six live trout Norm released into its waters,

snaps from the UK tour, the Guinness brewery in Dublin, the
view from a castle in Scotland,

the workaday mundane surroundings of a remote floating lumber camp: the cafeteria, austere bunk room, the bulletin board, all are back dropped by the majesty of coastal British Columbia,

Unlike those of us enslaved and taunted by the word Norm recognized the power, economy and superiority of pictures in Storytelling.

Chapter 37

Lingcod…

1.
We had one chance to fish for
these fanged, Bucketheaded, sweet fleshed,
"beautiful in their way," living fossils of the deep:
bouncing herring off the bottom near Race Point until
WHOOSH, then the weight, now
reel, reel, reel, reel,
reel, reel, reel, reel,
reel, reel, reel, reel.

Holy fuck Curtis, how far down are these mothers?

                                        Shut up and reel man!

Reel, reel, reel until Curtis scoops the coral
colored beast with a net, brings it on board for
photos (later it will be meat)   Jesus Kramer, smile!
A face only a mother could love.

He is not referring to the fish, gentle reader.

2.
By the way, that meat never made it East.

Ever inclined toward some of the most amazing feats
of organizational and co-ordination efforts to ensure the
hale and hearty army received their fair share of the
fishing spoils, Norm kept the ling meat, apologizing later
                            Sorry Kramer, the ling
                            never quite made it to the
                            Post Office. If it's any
                            consolation, it was
                            delicious.
To each man, God allows his version of crack cocaine.

Chapter 38

Cutthroat trout…

Beautiful, many hued small fry with big ideas trying to swallow
spinners meant for Coho salmon twenty times your size.

It reminds me of the Chicken Hawk cooking up
Foghorn Leghorn's foot in a frying pan
and of course our little maniac Napoleon.

Now that is a range of
references eh?

Chapter 39

Winner! Winner! Chicken Dinner!

In a spectacular display akin to Iron Mike
Tyson dropping Michael Spinks in 91
seconds, Cees de Jaeger the lineal verbal jousting
champion of our hale and hearty army has
been felled by the upstart American PFC Drucker
in the first round of The Rumble sort of
adjacent to or kind of near The Mighty Mighty Campbell at
Moxie's here in Campbell River, British Columbia
with a straight left comeback to the chin:

Ever heard of the widely read,
acclaimed, still quite relevant
business theorist Peter Drucker?
He's my grandfather.

Down goes de Jaeger!
Down goes de Jaeger!
Down goes de Jaeger!
Down goes de Jaeger!

Chapter 40

Poem for EWR…

I suppose gritty is the kindest, radio friendly adjective
I can pull from my mental word bag, my sweet Newark
Liberty International Airport. Remember my disappointment
when Air Canada switched servicing their non-stop YVR flight
from JFK to your crumbling self? Such cute, first world white
boy problems!

Still…I think it would be better if folks arriving from around
the globe walked into welcoming, clean, well lit arms
(like at YVR) and not your gritty, you really should have
flown somewhere else embrace.

You really have such potential darling, cease the fuck you and smile.

Chapter 41

Orca…

A small pod is frolicking up The Discovery Passage
north of Campbell River just off Painter's Lodge,
breaching, diving. It is fucking amazing.

And I wish I had a better camera than this shitty flip
phone to record this once in a lifetime sighting, but
no matter what I do it will not properly focus.

Of course, the many
rounds of Strongbow cider
may not be helping matters.

Witness, gentle reader, the juxtaposed upside and the
downside of being the first of our hale and hearty
army to arrive at the battleground: far too much empty
time, ready access to rushing rivers of liquor, the never
repeated sight of Orcas frolicking up The Passage and a
shitty flip phone for the unfocused recording thereof.

Chapter 42

Craig

The only other card carrying
member of the 4AM subset of our
hale and hearty army charged
with stripping away the bullshit and getting
down to the sweet, sweet, hazy essence.

Gentle reader if you feel I am being
evasive by means of brevity or omission
please contact your local representative
from the Central Intelligence
Agency and have them remand me to a
black site in Tunisia for rendition and a side
of waterboarding.

I ain't saying anything more unless tortured.

Chapter 43

A quick note about Norm's family…

Agnes and I are having our bi-monthly I
can trump that exchange on
family dysfunction and the usual
way that these chats ends is that
someone will invoke the clause/theorem:

O well we should not
complain all families are
fucked up

and with the certainty
of science the other would agree:

True enough.

But after myriad similar conversations
Agnes invoked the all families are
fucked up clause/theorem and I was
forced to counter:

You know that might not
be true because OK no
one from the outside can
speak with 100 percent
certainty about the inner
workings of any family unit
from outside said unit, but
from what I have seen,
eard and experienced
orm's family appears like
enuinely happy.

Further it appears that one can suffer chaos within one's own childhood and
NOT bequeath said chaos
to future generations.

Wow.

Indeed.

Chapter 44

The night at the Tyee Pub…

Is known for two things:

1.
The consumption of thirteen double
Bloody Caesars (the national cocktail
of Canada, when in Canada, gentle reader
when in Canada) by your
humble narrator who by the grace of the
river, forest and ocean gods remained somehow
upright and retained the ability to hold
suitable, cogent conversation and even
managed with Norm's reminder to call
Agnes before she went to bed back.

2.
In response to our bullying taunts about
his leaving the battle earlier than the rest
of us which surely was a sign of waning
masculinity and inability to hang with the
Big Dogs off the porch, Craig forwards the best
ever comeback via text message, a message which
makes it exceedingly clear that he his having a far
better evening than we are or will pretend to have
and the dregs of the hale and hearty army are forced to
capitulate simply, You win. Enjoy your night!

I will now allow you gentle reader adequate
time to give your imagination free reign regarding
the content of that text message.

Really? You have a dirty, dirty mind gentle reader.
I am shocked!

We might not be officers, but we are
gentlemen (sort of, mostly, kinda, OK not really
but even thieves possess an honor right?)

Chapter 45

Brown bear (grizzly)…

Curtis and Gene are debating exactly which
bear species could have the tracks left in
the sand bar

They're pretty damned big for a
lack bear eh Curtis?

I was thinking the same thing
Gino. Someone was telling me the
other day that there might be grizz
up here, but I didn't quite believe
him. There aren't supposed to be
brown bears on The Island.

These tracks say otherwise.

Let's keep our eyes open. We do
not mess with browns.

No we do not.

Some time later it proved true that
there was a brown bear (grizzly) working
that river. Yikes!

Judging by the size of tracks left in
the sand bar where we stopped
for lunch, (Holy fucking HUGE!)
I am thankful we never made
your acquaintance.

Go thee in peace Big Hands!

Chapter 46

Gene

Gene aka Gino aka the Gene Machine (OK I
do not believe that anyone in our hale and hearty
crew ever referred to Gene as the Gene Machine, but
I like it,) Gene is Curtis' partner in guide, cut from
a similar if wilder outdoorsman back to the land cloth.

When the power goes out entirely and the Apocalypse
comes nipping our noses I am going to Gene's house.

Chapter 47

One trip ends with a now famous quotation…

Part of our hale and hearty army is preparing
to depart Cam River via the airport while
the Vancouver area residents are readying
themselves for the drive down Highway 19
to Duke Point to catch the ferry back to
the mainland and we are making
rounds, shaking hands, congratulating those
who have fought the bravest battles, gently mocking
those who have fallen in the mighty might Campbell or broken
Curtis' expensive trolling rods, extending
If you ever find yourself in…invitations to
New York, Boston and maybe we will see you
next year when Dr. Les steps into the center of
the circle, commands everyone's
attention and in his own inimitable way says,
Gentlemen, zis was a fine trip indeed. Never have
I heard za word blowjob so many times used in
so many unique ways. I thank you. After a
round of laughter we left for the airport, the ferry because
after that nothing can be said which will matter
in the least and again the dregs of the hale and hearty
army must capitulate, You win Dr. Les. You win.
Have a good drive home.

Chapter 48

On hangovers…

I am wondering today
what the forays of the hale
and hearty army might have
looked like if my head were
clear of the hangovers, the
gauzy film, hammer to anvil, sour
teetering need pork
fat stat! stomach, Geezus I
best double down on the
Alka Seltzer and Dramamine
before hopping the Grady's rail today.

I reckon there would be a far
different tale to tell and none
of you would give a rat's ass to
hear it.

Besides, I am told that
one must suffer
for art.

Little doubt there
was suffering, I only
hope this is art.

Chapter 49

The mystery beast moving noisily through the riparian underbrush toward our present position…

We are amazing over the tracks of Big Hands, when
Curtis clips the conversation: Jesus! Guys shut the fuck
                                                   up a minute!

Something BIG, very BIG is moving noisily through the riparian
underbrush directly toward our present position.

What the hell is that?

Given that we have been just marveling over the day
old tracks of a fairly sizable grizzly bear, there is one
obvious, damned frightening answer to that question.

My mind is spinning out the wildlife options
that could be noisily through the riparian
underbrush toward our present position:

Is it Big Hands?	God I hope not.
A bull elk?	That would be cool.
A bull elk chasing off a juvenile pretender?	That would be cooler still.
Is it Big Hands?	God I hope not.
Big Hands in pursuit of a bull elk?	That would be AMAZING.
Is it Big Hands in pursuit of our raucous,	
hale and hearty crew redolent of hangover breath,	
yesterday's whiskey spills and meat	
farts too numerous to count?	God I hope not.

It's a…Hereford cow and her calf.

I am guessing that they did not get the memo that
Big Hands is prowling these parts.

My grandfather Earl was right, at least in part, we
have bred a mighty strain of dumb into beef cattle.

But perhaps the cattle apple does not fall
far from the interspeciel breeding tree.

That or it's awfully, awfully kind of the rancher to leave
Big Hands a succulent veal appetizer and a beefy entrée.

Dumb leaves the gate a 1 to 9 favorite.

Chapter 50

A long poem recollecting the nights of extreme overindulgence…
.
.
.
.
.
.
.
.
.
.
.
.
.
.
.
.
.
.
.
.
.
.
.
.
.
.
.
.
.
.
.
.
.
.
.
.
.
.

Dude, what the fuck did you expect?

Chapter 51

A few brief exercises and/or observations on forestry, dendrochronology, wood science and products…

1.
The term old growth Radiata ™ is an oxymoron.

Please explain why.

2.
Western red cedar is a riparian specie.

Please define the term riparian specie and where best in the broad forests of the Pacific Northwest would one look for Western red cedar trees.

3.
You can tell when a tug is hauling a boom of Western red cedar rather than hemlock, spruce or fir by the height of the logs in the boom.

Please explain.

4.
The cross section of the old growth Douglas fir at Forintek, UBC had growth rings of 1/16" or less.

Compare and contrast this with the growth profile of Radiata pine.

Chapter 52

October 9, 2013…

I recall this trip episodically devoid of time or linear continuity:

1.
Given the volume of business he is conducting
on The Island of late Norm had set up shop at Painter's,
there's a photo somewhere of a can of Kokanee, Glacier Fresh
Beer, sweating on the deck rail back dropped by an
ominous evening fog,

2.
Norm arcs a bear banger after we conclude our
river fishing expedition BAM and scares the
shit out of those who had their backs turned and
failed to see him extricate the device from his
waterproof pack. Me mostly,

3.
Ever the gadget guru, Norm passes around a newly
acquired satellite phone (cell reception cuts out a
few miles North of Cam River) and we all call home to
say hi honey I am calling you on a satellite phone from
the banks of the Forever Unnamed River (see Curtis?)

Ain't technology great?

4.
Two other members of the hale and hearty army, likely
taking into account what was best for me (never my strong
suit) have left me sitting in front of Painter's Lodge while
they grabbed a cab to downtown Campbell River. Norm and I share
a few digestives in the Fireside Lounge before we make the long walk up
the hill to the cabins. Odd what liquor does to distance and time,

5.
In crude duct tape lettering, JD and CAF have rechristened
the Grady *Lil' Ball Scarf* (the derivational root of this moniker

escapes me) and tainted the rail in the process as BB and I stood watch on the dock. Captains of mayhem we!

6.
For the first time ever, though threatened many times previously, we drop a couple of crab pots in Menzies Bay before
heading out to troll for silver. We'll pull a few Dungeness from the deep before I have to leave for the airport on the first leg home.

7.
I am thinking while the lines are taught behind the Grady, I do not know if I will make the trip next year. Maybe it's time to change it up.

8.
Norm and I shake hands at the Municipal Dock as the taxi cab driver loads my gear and boxes of frozen fish into the truck. I hand Norm a bottle of The MacAllan 18,

Thank you for everything Norm.

You're welcome, have a safe trip home and give my best to Agnes.

9.
Norm. Chilling in the lounge. Flight in 2 hours. How was last night? Saw CAF and the boys in the terminal and think I made the right move. chilled had a good room service meal and had a good rest. Thanks again for everything.

The boys stayed at Moxies and then sat with me in the painters lounge....,,,,,vey interesting.

Did you get the fish into a freezer?

Thanks for joining us!!!!!!!

Hotel had them on ice all night. So they should

be good. Curtis posted a bunch of pics of us from
yesterday. You should check out on Facebook
when you can. You home by now? Or ferrying?

On da ferry

You'll have to share details on the 'very interesting'
evening sometime. Safe waters home. Happy
Thanksgiving to you and Sandy and the
family. All the best!

Thank- you

Say hi to Agnes

Will do. How were the crabs?

Excellent

Have to do it next time when I can partake.
Yes, it was just BB, JD and I. Steamed for 7 minutes and then dipped in garlic
butter.

10.

Journey OK. Took day off.

Did the fish
survive?

It did. Coho looks awesome.
Like sockeye in color.
The chum will need extra seasoning…

Chapter 53

An introduction: A brief ode to rotting wood…

To think I was recruited into this hale and hearty
army due to a basic fact of science. To whit, when
exposed to prolonged periods of moisture especially those
that cause its moisture content to exceed 20%, wood
can and will support the growth of decay causing organisms.

I have met some of the best friends in
this perhaps any life and been witness to
the magic that is coastal
British Columbia because
wood
rots.

It is an odd, odd Life brother.

Chapter 54

The Lessons…

1.
Both feet over the side when
preparing to leave the raft.

I repeat both feet over the side when
preparing to leave the raft.

Despite the repetition I would require
empirical verification of this lesson before
becoming an I told you so
acolyte, scolding a new member
of the Campbell River Swim Club,
"Dude, really?"

2.
"Business first, then the wine," which
I have tweaked somewhat, "All business
will be conducted before the second bottle
is reduced to bitter tailings."

All Lessons should be subject to
empirical verification and necessary
adjustment based on one's own real
world experience.

Yes, that reeks of moral equivalency.

I am sorry sunshine, we live in a grey world.

3.
New recruits to the hale and hearty
army shall never tweak napping
veterans unless another veteran initiates
said tweaking.

Sometimes lessons are hard learned

O mighty VP of Acquisitions, overseas trade and
riverboat casinos.

4.
Don't feed the bears.

Shit. Sorry about that!

5.
Never, never, never challenge
a New Zealander to a drinking contest.

Holy giant booze absorbent
sponges with legs Batman!

I praise thee giant booze absorbent
sponges with legs!

Halest and heartiest of
our crew!

6.
Thirteen double bloody Caesars is
one too few
or
ten too many.

It all depends on what you wish to
subsequently undertake.

Too few if your goal is strip away
the bullshit and get down to the
sweet, bitter essence at 4AM.

Too many if you wish to pilot
your recently acquired riverboat
casino and dinner theater.

7. (aka DB's lessons)
Do not sit on
Curtis' very expensive
trolling rods.

8.
A fishing net can be used
for netting many things
beyond fish:
a 2-4 of Kokanee,
Glacier Fresh Beer,
tossed
one
at
a
time,
a split of
The Glenlivet,
giant chocolate chip cookies sealed
in Saran wrap and more hopefully:
DB when Curtis
hip checks him overboard
after sitting on the very expensive
trolling rods.

9.
I am sure CAF will second this lesson:

There is a serious downside to
stripping away the bullshit and getting
down to the sweet, sweet, hazy
essence at 4AM.

Breakfast at seven boys!
We're on the water by eight!

Fuck.

10.
The weather of coastal British Columbia
is widely variable, so bring layers, bring
variety and check your lame American
we can not possibly go out in this rain
attitude at the gate of the distal, distant
end of the Domestic terminal at YVR
because around these parts if we sat inside
every time it rained, threatened to rain or was
forecast to rain we would not leave the house for

thirteen months so we are going out hell, high
water and otherwise besides you absolutely
must see the way the forest cracks a glowing
green radiant smile after the rains
abate and the sun steals in, a sneak thief.

Part Two:

And thus to Buffalo

Chapter 55

And thus we went to Buffalo…

Chasing nostalgia, my favorite music of all
time and chicken wings, glorious, original hot
crispy Buffalo wings devoid of breading, barbeque
sauce, teriyaki infused, ranch dressing bullshit.

Eat whatever flavor of wings you want people, but
please stop calling them Buffalo wings dammit!

How I never in the course of thirty years
had ever managed to see a concert by the Cowboy
Junkies, could be a tale for another a time {or not.} At
any rate that is a long time to be a fan of a still touring,
remarkably durable band to never have seen even
one of their live shows and Agnes and I have made it a bit of mantra
that when something unique comes to our attention to just go
and not resort to excuses and reasons why not and so Agnes secured
tickets for their show at the Mary Seaton Room at Kleinhans Music Hall in
beautiful, decaying Buffalo for my birthday and this show was going to be
truly special because they were going to perform their seminal album
The Trinity Sessions front to back. Trinity Sessions the album
recorded live at Trinity Church in Toronto that began my obsession
with the band back in 1987/1988 when MB shared the album and said
I think you will like this dark, sad one. She was very right on both accounts.

Shall we speculate that Agnes' gift to be the best birthday present ever?
I cannot say for certain, we'll have a straw poll on my death bed, but
surely in the running especially for me, quite possibly the
worst gift recipient of all time, in a line of grouchy bad gift
recipients who always respond to what do you want for (fill in the blank)
your birthday?
Christmas?
our anniversary?
with a stock response I don't need or want anything really, maybe
a package of socks and underwear if you HAVE to get me something.

Because people gifts are boomerangs, booby traps, land mines, tiger pits

filled with excrement smeared pongee stakes. I have seen gifts turn
happy people instantly sad. I have seen gifts dissemble, destroy and in all
honesty, I have never been sadder than after my Aunt Helene passed away
and I
was given the small fractured, imperfect poem I had framed and gifted her
some ten years previous. ugh. Transience, loss, sadness all spun
together in a dusty 5x7 frame. Even now, I am getting teary thinking
about it. So instead we must onward hale and hearty ones ever onward
to happier shores of chicken wings, sweeter nostalgias and the music of the
Cowboy Junkies.

Chapter 56

Duff...

The signs outside of Duff's, inside of Duff's and on the
T-shirt uniforms all staff wears say:

Warning!
Medium is hot!
Medium hot is very hot!
Hot is very very hot!

Color it cowardice and the result of some research on the
Internet (technology is great ain't it?) but we order medium, extra
crispy wings, French fries and a half pitcher of Pepsi (I know, beer
next time I swear.) Our order arrives and we quickly
discover that this warning unlike similar verbiage
Agnes and I dismiss as warnings for white bread
America is utterly and completely true. The chicken wings
are indeed HOT, extra crispy, absolutely perfect and we
have picked the perfect time to indulge, 1PM on
Thursday October 24, 2013 and we
finish our pile of perfect wings, small French
fries and a half pitcher of Pepsi (I know, beer
next time I swear) before the happy hour crowd
descends and we're back before 3PM on Thursday
October 24 with Eli and Angie safe, cozy at the
Red Roof Inn outside of Buffalo and ready for a long
post gorging pre-Cowboy Junkies show nap.

A perfect start to the day gentle
reader a perfect start.

Chapter 57

The show...

Was superb
and I will not
bore you with
a long fan boy
explanation of the
nuance and complexity
of the set list with myriad
footnotes, attributions and
observations because in truth
all I could do was listen to the
music, awestruck, alternating, nods,
smiles perhaps a tear or two through
the first set of new music and the
second Trinity Sessions set and I
walked from the Mary Seaton
Room at the Kleinhans Music Hall into
the beautiful Buffalo night one
of the happiest humans ever to tread
this great, green Earth, knowing we
still had two days of our mini-vacation
left and the wide arms of friends and family
anticipating our arrival in the once
mighty Cap D.

The sleep of the dead came readily that
night in the Red Roof Inn outside of
Buffalo that night, I still recall myself
smiling before the pulsing, shimmering
swirl of sleep came for me.

Chapter 58

The set list fanboy poems…

Of course I can't not provide you all
with the set list and accompanying fan boy
notations, etc. and etc.:

Date: October 23, 2013
Band: Cowboy Junkies
Venue: Mary Seaton Room in Kleinhans Music Hall
                    Buffalo, NY

Set 1

Is a quick and nimble run of new music mostly from the 2012 multi-disc
release Nomad Series and 2013's Kennedy Suite

  1.   See You Around, Nomad Series Disc 2 "Demons," Vic Chesnutt
       cover from About to Choke, 1996,

What? A whole disc of Vic Chesnutt covers? By the Cowboy Junkies?
Mental note: Purchase Nomad Series at first opportunity.
So suggestible and easily led. I know.

2.   Ladle, Nomad Series Disc 2 "Demons," Vic Chesnutt cover from
About to Choke, 1996,

A single warm tear traces slow serpentine toward the safe
anonymity of graying beard. Odd because this is a raucous,
rocking cover of Ladle a ragged, rocking song. Never trust a tear.

3.   Late Night Radio, Nomad Series Disc 3, "Sing in my Meadow,"
4.   3rd Crusade, Nomad Series Disc 3, "Sing in my Meadow,"

What a tight and amazing group of musicians. Maybe
I should ask them to join my band.

5.   Damaged from the Start, Nomad Series Disc 4, "The Wilderness,"

Liking these new tunes. Quite a lot, but no disrespect…I need The Trinity.

6.	We are the Selfish Ones, <u>Nomad Series</u> Disc 4, "The Wilderness,"
7.	Fairytale, <u>Nomad Series</u> Disc 4, "The Wilderness,"
8.	Take Heart, <u>Kennedy Suite</u>.

Buy KSuite? Maybe. If we have some miles on Amex or a lonely Amazon gift card.

Set 2

<u>The Trinity Session</u>, 1988, in its entirety:

1.	Mining for Gold,
2.	Misguided Angel,
3.	Blue Moon Revisited (Song for Elvis,)
4.	I Don't Get It,
5.	I'm So Lonesome I Could Cry,
6.	To Love is to Bury,
7.	200 More Miles,
8.	Dreaming My Dreams with You,
9.	Working on a Building,
10.	Sweet Jane
11.	Postcard Blues
12.	Walkin' After Midnight.

Part Three:

When last we left our heroes

Chapter 59

The instant of heart break…

These transformational moments find
us though we have taken measures to confuse
and evade, keeping to the secondary
roadways, driving across three states, registering
under an assumed name at the Red Roof Inn outside
of Buffalo, prowling the city anonymous,
unannounced, employing a strict cash only
rule for procuring the necessary supplies.

These transformational moments find
us in swirling clouds of happiness, of
satisfaction and of reveling for seven
seconds in the transient, ethereal
warmth of unmitigated joy.

These transformational moments find
us beneath a sky so blue, an atheist might
for a fractioned second think, "Well, maybe…"

These transformational moments find
us plying the New York State Thruway just
east of Utica on the downgrade into Herkimer.

These transformational moments find
us at the Indian Castle rest stop because
I knew the missed call, your voice mail on
the work cell could not be good news and I
did not want to do something intentionally
absent minded like walk into west bound traffic.

These transformational moments find
us. God fucking damn it.
The instant of heart break (original)

1.
Beneath the deepest blue sky, a perfect

autumn day, east of Utica on the New York State
Thruway riding the straightaway
just before the curving downgrade into
Herkimer, a voice mail pops up on the work
cell phone, distracted I think, "Jesus Christ! Why the
hell does this thing seem to only ring when
it chooses to? I'm sure it's a setting or some
damned thing I'll have to check with IT…" but then
mid-useless thought the realization shit hits the
rotary mind oscillator, "You IDIOT nobody ever CALLS these
days unless it's bad, bad news."

Agnes has trouble making out the message, but
I know the voice, it's clipped almost military
cadence and cool brevity:
Kramer
Flynn
911
call me back
ASAP.

OK, so I can't just pull over on the side
of the road, make this call, maybe lose my
shit and walk into traffic or something
equally stupid. Where's the next rest stop?
Just eat of the Little Falls exit, I'll pull in and
call, but FUCK what happened? who? where? why?

There is an almost, dare I say, gentle
ache deep in the left side of my chest.

Chapter 60

No more…

In the instant after Craig
said,   Norm's gone. His
    float plane went down off
    The Island.
I remember thinking, no more, and then flashing
images cascading, a slideshow with narration and dude this
is so fucked up, the narrator has a clearly British accent,
                                                    (mentally ill much?)
no more wildlife snapshots,
no more philosophical moments beneath
a cold drizzling October rain,
no more hale and hearty army,
no more spills into the mighty, mighty Campbell,
no more childish antics or gentlemanly exchanges,
no more sage business plans,
no more plying the backwaters of The
Island hungover like a motherfucker,
no more
no more
no more
no more Norm.

My gauzed revelry ended when my
conscience returned to the helm, a
hard MMA truth elbow to the jaw,   You selfish little bitch.
    You may have lost a friend, a mentor even
                                                    but others have lost
                                                    so much
                                                    more.

O my God Sandy, Gail, Lisa.

                                                    Exactly.

And harsh scathing guilt overtook
the British inflected image
cascade and wedged it into

the ditch,
      to think of yourself while

It is so like you

others suffer.
What the fuck dude?

What the fuck indeed because while this
entire scene and interaction with my bitch
ass conscience plays out in my mind I continue
to hold an almost phone conversation with Craig

They do not know what
happened yet, but they
were puddle jumping clear
cuts off Port Hardy and
the float plane

      went down.

But we just saw him last week.   I know.
But…   I know.
But…   I know.
Well, fuck.   I know.
Shit.   I know.
OK…well please send Sandy and the
girls our sincerest condolences and let
me know what the arrangements
are. I will be there. Be well brother.   Will do. I'm out.

And I do not know exactly how
this poem should end because
for me it has not ended as
yet and I am beginning to
wonder if it ever will.

Well fuck. Shit.   I know.

You will never be ready.

Chapter 61

Friday October 25, 2013, Part One

Please advise regarding the protocols for the moments after receiving tragic news.
I am uncertain how one proceeds.

Do you totally lose your shit and walk into eastbound traffic on the New York State Thruway?

Seek something very sharp and start cutting?

Pull clumps of hair from your head until rendered bald but for a tuft at your forelock?

Repeatedly punch something inanimate with bone cracking intent?

Fall to your knees and begin wailing?

Lay and curl fetal in the parking lot and say absolutely nothing for three days and nights?

It seems not.

You get back in your car albeit stunned like a steer before
the delivering blade, a small tear creasing your left ventricle.

You cannot quite place the pain's source at once
it is sharp distinct, then a general gnawing ache.

Still you ply the Thruway past
the familiar, once mighty now skidding
mill towns and cities of the Mohawk:
Canajoharie
Sharon Springs
Fonda
Fultonville
Amsterdam to Schenectady
for an excellent Moroccan meal with

one of your best friends in this and perhaps
all subsequent lifetimes.

You eat picholine olives marinated in
harrisa redolent of chile, luscious
lamb and drink hot mint tea.

You smile, reveling in the reconnection while
the tear in your left ventricle spiders across your heart.

You wait hope even crave the delivering blade.

Chapter 62

Friday October 25, 2013, Part Two

Since 11:32AM EDT, everything reminds me
of Norm, Sandy's husband, Gail and Lisa's
father, our departed Lat/Czech/Canadian
generalissimo, mentor, friend:

Some things for no reason at all say an insipid radio friendly
song by Coldplay for instance. Fucking shoot me.

Some for deep and specific reasons like today's sky
which is a spectacular Coastal British Columbia
blue, the blue that followed hours, upon hours, upon
hours of dark autumn monsoon, the Tim Burton
Halloween notebook I bought for Agnes when
we stopped at Walgreen's for ZiCam leaving
Buffalo still naïve and joyous, a campaign
sign in Schenectady:

GATTAN
FINN
FLUMAN
for County Legislature

spins me into revelry and recollection:

Because gentle reader Finn is Curtis' springer
spaniel. Finn loves fishing more than Curtis I
suspect, barking as we attempt a successful
silver retrieve, barking as we steer the silver
boatward, barking as Curtis brings the flapping beast
to the deck with a deft flick and lift of net, barking
as the fish is dispatched (reader discretion advised) with
an oaken WHACK, a now silent Finn licking the slowly
pooling blood behind silver gills before the fish
is hoisted, tilted just so to catch
the sun, the moment properly recorded.   Geezus! Smile Kramer!

At ebb tide and times Norm would goad

Finn into a growling barking showdown on the
deck or Finn would soak the sun
curled next to Norm. It ain't snitching
to say there was often a nap involved. Finn
doing what dogs do best and most often. Norm
taking the sleep inducing rays for their
rumored restorative properties.

I smile without direction,
I want to walk into traffic,
seek something sharp and start cutting,
pull clumps of hair from my head,
punch something inanimate over and over,
fall to my knees and begin wailing.

Instead I smile and we check into the fabulous
Microtel on Route 7 in Latham, NY.

Great gods of commerce, these rooms are small.

Chapter 63

Friday October 25, 2013, Part Three, becomes Saturday October 26, 2013…

We are back at the fabulous Microtel
on Route 7 in Latham, NY

Great gods of commerce,
these rooms are still small.

I have returned with a suitable supply
to bring sleep: cider, beer, disgustingly
sweet malt beverages that under normal life
conditions never, ever cross my lips

If you must know I could
not make up my fucking mind and I am apparently incapable of sound
decision making.

Is this grief? Shock? The warning signs of a psychic break? We shall see
gentle reader. We shall
see.

I have also bought bags of salty
snacks for my long standing tradition
of eating my feelings, but I do not
eat or drink or sleep.

Instead I play the Vancouver Island
CBC news broadcast at very low volume

I do not want to wake
Agnes, selfishly and for her
sake and well selfishly.

on the phone over
and
over
and
over.

We begin with a
developing story off
Vancouver Island. A small
float plane has crashed in a
remote area along the
Central Coast.

The aircraft went down
about one hundred
kilometers North of
Campbell River.

Police confirm that all
three people aboard were
killed.

I make a gesture toward the preferred
emptiness of inebriation and crack a cider, a beer and
a disgusting malt beverage that under normal life
conditions never, ever crosses my lips.

They go warm, flat and undiminished.

I search the web for news about the accident

Three men are dead after a
float plane crashed on a
small, remote island east of
northern Vancouver Island
Thursday morning.

Their identities have not
been released.

Technology sure is great ain't it?

I do not sleep or eat or drink. Instead I
play the Vancouver Island
CTV news broadcast at very low
volume on the phone over
and
over
and
over.

Kerry Adams (verify
spelling) joins us now with
an update on the deadly
float plane accident off
Vancouver Island.
Kerry…

Well Tamara all three people who were on board that plane have died.

The crash happened on West Cracroft Island off the Northeast tip of
Vancouver Island.

The pilot and passengers have not been publicly identified.

I search the web for news about the accident.

Three men are dead after a float plane crashed on a small, remote island east of northern Vancouver Island Thursday morning.

Their identities have not been released.

Technology sure is great ain't it?

At 5AM, I sleep as if sedated for open heart surgery.

By 7AM, I am up. I pour the stale room temperature cider, beer and disgusting malt beverage into the sink.

I play the Vancouver Island CBC news broadcast at very low volume (I do not want to wake Agnes) on the phone one more time.

We begin with a developing story off Vancouver Island.

A small float plane has crashed in a remote area along the Central Coast.

The aircraft went down about one hundred kilometers North of Campbell River.

Police confirm that all three people aboard were killed

I search the web for news about the accident.

Three men are dead after a float plane crashed on a small, remote island east of northern Vancouver Island Thursday morning.

Their identities have not been released.

Technology sure is great ain't it?

I pack up the suitable, slightly reduced supply
of cider, beer, saccharin, disgusting malt
beverages and the unopened bags of salty snacks.

I wake up Agnes and we ready the menagerie
for the drive home through a world
that is achingly similar to
the world of Wednesday
October 23, 2013 except

Three men are dead after a
float plane crashed on a
small, remote

island east of northern Vancouver
Island Thursday morning.

Their identities have not been
released.

And even more than yesterday,
I want to walk into traffic,
seek something sharp and start cutting,
pull clumps of hair from my head,
punch something inanimate over and over,
fall to my knees and begin wailing.

Instead I drive the menagerie home.

I have work on Monday.

Chapter 64

Forestry poem II…

This only occurred to me as I spoke
with Sandy, back home on Sunday
October 27, 2013 we forget as we build
these houses, sit on chairs, clean
up the floor beneath the baby and
her bowl of spaghetti in marinara, pollute
pure white paper with poetry and wipe
our asses that these everyday, mundane things
result from the most dangerous
jobs in North America and that
people are mangled, lose fingers, toes
and limbs, are permanently
disabled and DIE, so that we can build
houses, sit on chairs, clean
up the floor beneath the baby and
her bowl of spaghetti in marinara, pollute
pure white paper with poetry and wipe
our asses.

Chapter 65

This is not a poem. I repeat this is not a poem.

Aviation Investigation A13P0278

On 24 October 2013, a Cessna 185 floatplane, operated by CBE Construction, doing business as Air Cab, was reported to have crashed on an island in Potts Lagoon, West Cracroft Island, British Columbia. There were 3 persons on board, and all were fatally injured. There was no post-impact fire.

And there you have it.

Chapter 66

Crossing international borders...

Reason for entering Canada today?

Celebration of Life Service for
a friend taken suddenly in a tragic float
plane accident two weeks ago.

I am very sorry for your loss.
Welcome to Canada.

Chapter 67

The service…

The Victory Memorial Park Funeral Centre is
packed, the staff has set up chairs
any where there is unutilized
floor space:
in the vestibule,
in the aisles,
in a small room
adjoining the chapel.

I settle into my chair next to Craig and Heather, ensure
I have turned off my cell phone and slide it into my
pocket with the travel pack of tissues Agnes thoughtfully
packed. I envy Craig's (Heather's??) dark sunglasses, a strong, stoic, concealing
move. My glasses conceal nothing and soon enough
I am reaching for the travel pack of tissues Agnes thoughtfully
sent, trying to hide my rolling grief with
discreet dabs as the pastor opens the
service and then
Rob and
Gail and
Lisa
share wonderful
stories and canyons of loss.

As the First Nations representative (name? title?)
sings a song of transition, tells
how Norm always knew the best
places to eat and ends by saying
that his grandchildren and their
grandchildren and their grandchildren
will know Norm's name my cell phone
rings (a well meaning friend from
back East forgetting the time zone
thing is checking in on me.)

Ain't technology great?

I am officially THAT guy. I had turned the phone back
on while fishing for the travel pack of tissues Agnes
thoughtfully packed.

Though now I am cursing:
her thoughtfulness,
my well meaning friend from back East,
the fact that I did not bring my concealing
dark sunglasses and I am THAT guy whose
cell rang at Norm's service
but really I am cursing these canyons of loss,
transition and the scales of Life that
must return to equilibrium.

Chapter 68

Hey Norm, what's good in British Columbia?

I am sure that we will be alright,
everyone has been telling us so since
October 24, 2013. And we have been
lying to convince ourselves ever since.

I am sure we will be alright
because the shaman chanted
a transition prayer that made
us weep and told us your name
will live for a thousand years.

I am sure we will be alright, but
I keep wanting to call, e-mail, text
to say, "Hey Norm, what's good in
British Columbia?"

I am sure that we will be alright, but
I cannot say the same for several small
items around this house or the
light switch in Craig's hallway. Man
Axiom 17: If something cannot be
fixed, something else must be broken.

I am sure that we will be alright once
every little fucken thing does not send
a jolting, burning surge into our hearts:
an e-mail solicitation from Air Canada,
when Quicken seeks to autofill Sandpiper Bar into
the register every time I add a transaction starting
with "S," when I am prepping a filet of chum salmon for
a new Goan fish curry I have been wanting to try, when
I am driving to work and really should pull over and give
myself a moment because I cannot quite see the road, when I
think of a fine autumn day in Buffalo,
Duff's, chicken wings,
The Cowboy Junkies,

The Trinity Session,
blue skies,
joy, sadness,
liberation, but
now guilt
too.

I am sure we will be alright once we
can find a way to banish this guilt, this
feeling of usurping tragedy because others
have
lost
so
much
more.

I am sure that we will be alright once we
can stop firing out of bed at 1:21 AM to
write this poem or turn on the Cartoon
Network or sit in an empty bathtub and
try to read away this insomniac ache.

I am sure we will be alright in
1 week,
30 days,
6 months,
1 year,
5 years,
10 years,
50 years.
It's like the lottery. Pick one.

I am sure that we will be alright.
As of this past Saturday we
have officially drunk enough
to fill this deep, deep psychic hole five
times over. Coming to a theater
near you: "six times over."

I am sure we will be alright once
we have the report and it is
definitively determined exactly what the
fuck happened over Pott's Lagoon,

West Cracroft Island, British Columbia,
Canada on October 24, 2013.

I am sure we will be alright.
You know what?
Fuck that!

We may move on, we may play nice like good little
childrens, we may say all the right things about
finding peace and acceptance, but we will never be alright!

The best we can hope for is being alright
with not being alright, accepting that
there will always be a part of us that
is broken, allowing that because we were
loved the law of reciprocity dictates that you
were loved and while our hearts may still
function in the medical sense the sliver you took with you
on October 24, 2013 will ensure we never feel alright
because we are no longer ALL HERE.

And I still want to call, e-mail, text
to say, "Hey Norm, what's good in
British Columbia?"

Chapter 69

Even in Death instruction…

1.
After the service Cees and Craig and Curtis and I were
questioning what the remaining members of the
hale and hearty army would do without our
beneficent generalissimo and I mentioned
that when faced with a difficult life or business
event, I had begun asking myself,
What Would Norm Do? or WWND? if
you are into brevity, acronyms or need something
that will better fit on a T-shirt.

WWND? has aided in the sailing of these shitty
psychic seas of the last sixteen months,

WWND? has held me from harm,
walking into traffic,
securing something sharp and cutting,
pulling clumps of hair from my head,
punching something inanimate over and over,
falling to my knees and wailing.

WWND? has allowed me to better recognize the pretenders,

WWND? made me pull to the side of the road when grief
rolled hot from my eyes while driving to work,

WWND? Lead me to GAGA, a mantra based on Norm's
method for addressing complex matters business and otherwise:

Gather requisite information
Analyze information gathered
Generate conclusions based on the analysis of the information gathered
Act upon the conclusions generated by the analysis of the information
gathered.

WWND? and GAGA are actually this collection's raison d'être

because
WWND? became WWKD? and Kramer writes (sort of) poems and
so Kramer would write a poem about Norm
but because
after sixteen months
of gathering, analyzing, re-analyzing,
failed attempts, false starts, missed
ferry connections and
generally getting no where
fast or at all
it was exceedingly
clear that a singular poem could
never possibly contain, summarize or
explain Norm, so WWND?
He'd write a fucking book.

2.
Carpe diem motherfuckers (babies?) carpe diem, trust the
future as little as possible because you never
know when multiple modifications will alter
the performance of the modified airframe resulting
in an aerodynamic stall at an unrecoverable
altitude and everything
just
Ends.

Chapter 70

Fucken Norm…

Is a phrase Craig and I now
toss into our conversations
when loss or sadness or
a bitter cocktail of both (a twist of guilt
if you please barkeep) exceeds then
overwhelms
our ability or desire to explain or share or
discuss further even in the sweet
sweet hazy essence of 4AM when
all things should be stripped and examined.

Fucken Norm.

Is the executioner of nostalgia, the arbiter of silent
ceaseless moments brooding above stale, increasingly
watery drinks. We are four hundred million miles
from our present position on planet Earth untethered
lost until one of us signals the return home.

Those San Francisco Giants could go all the way this year.

Chapter 71

Horseshoe Bay, British Columbia…

Agnes and I are watching the television
re-boot/prequel of Psycho, packaged by
the Arts and Entertainment Network as
The Bates Motel when I see a familiar
large bronze maritime propeller behind
Vera Famiga while she angrily stalks
the streets of small town
Oregon, USA as Norma Bates.

I say to Agnes,

I've been there. That's not
Oregon. It's the Village of
Horseshoe Bay, British Columbia.
Norm and I went there after we
missed the 12:30 ferry. We walked
into town for an unremarkable
lunch and ice cold Kokanees,
Glacier Fresh Beer, with George
and Dana before catching the 3PM
to Nanaimo for the two hour drive
up Highway 19 to Cam River.
Geezus that must have been 2008.

Now that I think about it, there might have
been photos in front of the familiar
large bronze propeller.

Odd that a life lived in orderly consecutive
increments of time becomes
chaos and
collage.

It has been
471 days
19 hours
27 minutes
and 42 seconds

since Craig's 911
voice mail on October
25, 2013 at 11:32AM, but this
morning it seems
like last Friday.

I read recently that American Psychiatric
Association in its definitive Diagnostic
and Statistical Manual of Mental
Disorders (DSM-V) has listed
persistent complex bereavement
disorder (PCBD) as a condition
for further study.

Given the condition's one year limitation

Stupid question: Does one
get an additional day if the
'event' occurs in a leap
year?

on grief for adults and these
subsequent chaotic
471 days
19 hours
27 minutes
and 42 seconds
I could receive said diagnosis and no
doubt a pill for the treatment
thereof and a bill for hours of talk
therapy or we could consider (which
medicine, like the clothing industry
fails to) that people are widely variable
and one size fits all solutions fail
always and it just takes some longer
to assimilate the chaos of tragedy.

I'm just saying.

I do wonder if there were any
photos taken with the large
bronze propeller, we took aim
and shot everything else.

It was a damned cool propeller.

Chapter 72

Reminders…

In case you were wondering Norm, I rarely
make it through a day without something
tripping the way back machine into whirring
action. There are the most common occurrences:

the First Nations totem pen I bought for Agnes at Gifts
of the Raven in the airport on my first trip
to Vancouver, the ink always runs out after five
words or less, I should look into a suitable refill,

the touting e-mails from Air Canada Seat sale! Save
on flights to Canada, Asia and Australia…that I receive
ever since I booked the flight West for your service. I just
cannot bring myself to follow the opt out link,

whenever the Vancouver Canucks are playing one of the locals or
I catch their game highlights on one of the sport news
networks or see the score on the crawling news ticker,

the Quicken account always asks to autofill
Sandpiper Pub into the payee slot whenever
I type the letter "S." Craig, Heather and I made
a few trips there in the painful, empty time expanses around
dinner with Sandy, Gail and Lisa and your service. Honestly,
I can't really recommend the place, but you probably knew that,

every time I make Goan or Madras fish curry or Thai salmon cakes with
a fillet of chum or pink still resident in the recesses of our freezers or flake
the pepper smoked chum from High Tide into a salad with sour
cream, mayo, dill, chives, lemon and fresh cracked black pepper,

whenever I open the front closet to reveal the canvas tool bag you left
in my care containing the basics of the claims inspections craft, please
review the poem "A man and his tools," if you require detail gentle reader
there seems little sense in repetition,

the 2010 Vancouver Games refrigerator magnets, the smiling mascots:
Quatchi, the Sasquatch with blue earmuffs,

Miga, mélange of spirit bear and Orca,
Sumi, half black bear half Thunderbird and their
Vancouver Island marmot sidekick MukMuk. Four mascots? I have
made a note that we must conduct the following
debate: Inclusion and Accommodation, aka the chunky stew
immigration model, Canadian political art or folly?

And then there are the random lightning strikes of recognition,
a smile and (too quickly) a dark sadness:

Whistler pamphlets in the cascading rack at
the Adria Hotel and Conference Center in
Bayside, Queens (Agnes is competing
in a Scrabble tournament,)

the bottle of Balzams on a high shelf at a gin joint
six blocks from my house,

the pawless, prosthetics wearing dog on last
night's Animal Planet show was named: Norman,

reading The New Yorker book review for The Goddess Pose, a biography about
Indira Devi, nee Eugenia Vassilievna, actress, socialite, yoga
instructor to Greta Garbo and Gloria Swanson, native of Latvija.

nine die when a DeHavilland DHC-3T Otter float plane crashes in Alaska,

watching the Haunted Passenger episode of Supernatural and identifying
the escalator entry and skyway to the Fairmont Hotel at YVR, the largely
empty, untrammeled waiting area beneath it where I sat killing time
waiting for the flight back to
EWR after your life celebration
service,

we drive by the house on the horse farm off Roanoke
Avenue owned by that very nice couple embroiled in
a lawsuit with their builder because their expensive home is
falling the fuck apart and after seeing your exceptional diligence in
inspecting the rotting trim on the house they want to hire you to fight
the builder, but instead you had some well considered, experientially
based advice that they were hell bent on not following, spend
your money to fix your house and drop the suit, you are throwing

good money after bad, the lawyers will bleed you dry and in the unlikely event you recoup anything from the builder, it will neither offset the attorney fees, the cost of repairing your home or the time spent. I will wager the suit is still in process these many, many years later.

Of course, poem boy if the goal were the quiet sands
of blissful forgetting writing a book might not
be the road one chooses to drive.   True
enough.

Chapter 73

Hockey update…

You would have been so proud of your
scrappy Latvian national hockey
team Norm, beating the Swiss to make
the quarter finals at the Sochi Olympics,
pushing the mighty Canadian
squad to the limit before a late goal
by Shea Weber felled the upstarts 2-1.

Kristers Gudlevskis' performance was
transcendent. He made 55 saves on
57 shots.

I cannot believe that was a year ago
last Thursday.

Time is whore and Madonna.

Chapter 74

The report…

I had been haunting the National Transportation Safety Board's website since November, 2013 checking to see if the report had been released.

I had been haunting the National Transportation Safety Board's website since November, 2013 checking to see if the report had been released with nothing to show for the effort beyond the cold hard facts:

On 24 October 2013, a Cessna 185 floatplane, operated by CBE Construction, doing business as Air Cab, was reported to have crashed on an island in Potts Lagoon, West Cracroft Island, British Columbia. There were 3 persons on board, and all were fatally injured. There was no post-impact fire.

I had been haunting the National Transportation Safety Board's website since November, 2013 checking to see if the report had been released with nothing to show for the effort beyond another view of the smiling face of Neil Hughes, lead investigator.

I had been haunting the National Transportation Safety Board's website since November, 2013 checking to see if the report had been released because I wanted to stay out in front of this, to not be caught unaware or in an opportune life moment because I wanted to be ready because there is no crying in cubicle farms.

And so I was surprised on Thursday February 26 to receive an e-mail from Craig with the simple title: Not cool and a link to a story in the Vancouver Sun "Float plane crashed, killing three, because pilot unfamiliar with modified airplane: TSB"

You will never be ready.

Chapter 75

An observation…

I must say Norm were you not one of the fatally
injured subjects of this report, you would be very
impressed with the efforts of Mr. Hughes at the
NTSB, very impressed indeed.

Chapter 76

Poem for Frederick Gerald Cecil Wiley, 40, of Merville...

Hello Mr. Wiley, please be advised if there's a Moxie's in Heaven or a similar sort of fast casual, TGIFridays-esque-ish joint with decent apps and a well stocked bar, the hale and hearty army will be trickling in over the next few decades or so.

In the interim, I submit the following ten items for your consideration:

1. Norm likes frozen Bellinis. Do not listen to him if says he does not or does not drink the one you order. Keep ordering until they're lined up like fence posts or until Doctor Les arrives,

2. Advice? Ignore Norm's prodding and subtle challenge, do not drink the Balzams,

3. To repeat, Do not drink the Balzams,

4. Tell Norm when you see him, that he is missed in ways we never dreamed possible,

5. 1 to 9, the same can be said about you,

6. Until we meet for the first time, rest well brother because once the hale and hearty army begins to array its ranks on the stools around you, the peaceful times of universal contemplation are officially concluded, the verbal jousting, pointed exchanges regarding familial heritage, lack of facility in Life, poor angling ability and penchant for cross dressing shall commence,

7. You might want to start practicing your verbal jousting. Norm will help. You probably know that he can't not help,

8. Do not drink the Balzams,

9. Do not drink the Balzams,

10. Do not drink the Balzams.

Yes gentle reader, I know there are
only five unique items. I can count. The
Balzams thing requires repetition and staunch
adherence to the recommendation.

I mean...have you tasted it?

Chapter 77

Poem for the pilot…

I
forgive
you.
Kevin
Williams.

Your boss
is another
matter
entirely.

Chapter 78

Poem for Cessna C-FQGZ…

Sure you were just a soulless machine, but
I can't imagine it was ever in your plans to
emulate stone and drop out of the sky on a remote
steep hill off West Cracroft Island or to have your
serviceable parts removed like salvaged organs for
eventual transplant or your remnant, twisted, shattered,
bits cast to the fickle, distant, recycling winds.

No one will weep for a soulless machine, but
they will surely curse you, especially once the
attorneys descend.

Chapter 79

Poem for the owner/operator of Air Cab of Coal Harbour, British Columbia…

I think Norm, as a fair minded businessman with a long history that touched every aspect (from stump to claim settlement) of the second most dangerous industry in North America and generalissimo of our little hale and hearty army would legally sign off on the following assessment:

Point the first:

A business owner's first responsibility is the safety
of all involved parties, more specifically his
employees and customers.

Point the second:

New employees should always be placed in
positions where safety and success are
guarantees not guess work.

Analysis:

Epic
Fail.

Chapter 80

Realization…

It has taken me sixteen months and a rather
unpleasant life experience to finally realize that there
will never be another generalissimo like Norm.

There will be pretenders, poseurs, good time
Charlies who in their selfish vision will fail
utterly as leaders and never recognize it.

Who will never have the knack to know precisely
when a night is a night, the party over, we must live
to fight another day boys and make it sound like the best
idea, your idea, everyone's idea to head home for
nightcaps and meat snacks at the main cabin.

Who know that 'no man left behind' is not
just for the United States Marine Corps, but
the responsibility of every generalissimo every
where even if their hale and hearty army is
comprised of ten less than fit for military
service denizens of the building materials
business.

Who know that all soldiers are to return home
to the world in one weary, still hung-over, now jet
lagging, joyous piece.

It has taken me sixteen months and a rather
unpleasant life experience to finally realize that there
will never be another generalissimo like Norm.

Unless perhaps?

No, I am at best a buck private in
the hale and hearty army always
on the edge of discharge for conduct
Unbecoming.

Chapter 81

Norm loved gadgets and tools:

1. His Big Johnson.

It's a tape measure gutter minded gentle reader, a
tape measure made by the Johnson Level and Tool
Manufacturing Company of Mequon, Wisconsin if you
must know. But, like you my friend, Norm loved to play
with the obvious double entendre:

Steve, please hand me my Big Johnson,
Well sir, I'll have to whip out my Big Johnson and see if that board
meets clearance requirements,
Excuse me ma'am, but this job will require my Big Johnson,
Steve please hold the dumb end of my Big Johnson at the
centerline of that porch post.

So, Norm was bereft a year or so later when I opened his tool
case and it was sans Big Johnson. Norm, what happened to your
Big Johnson? It broke Mr. Kramer, I broke my Big Johnson and
the Johnson Level and Tool Manufacturing Company of
Mequon, Wisconsin has renamed it the Big J. I don't
want a Big J. Big J is something someone who smokes
marihuana would seek. I want a Big Johnson.   I see your point.

2. Titanium hammers, pry bars, & etc.

Norm bought the best, always, and titanium tools fit the bill
perfectly. Also, it transforms the sadly banal into something Space Age when
you say, "Please hand me the titanium headed hammer and pry bar,"
you could be working on the International Space Station not
pulling a rotten, poorly installed piece of wood trim from a poorly
constructed structure that someone paid WAY too much money for.

Of course, titanium tools also made his tool case far lighter than
had he brought the conventional low tech forged steel equivalent
for each and every tool in the case, so we can have a hearty debate
on extravagance versus practicality and the International Space Station.

3. Infrared Ray (IR) camera.

Eye voodoo machine that proved just how poorly a structure was constructed, that someone paid WAY too much money for, more precisely it used the differential heat signatures of wet and dry building materials to illustrate the path of water flowing into (not always out of) a building envelope.

I like the sound of eye voodoo machine better and people these days may be more likely to believe it an oracle than the science behind it.

All Hail the Eye Voodoo Machine seer of the unseen! All Hail!

4. LL Bean Pathfinder LED cap.

Norm gifted Agnes this cap one year and I thought what would
we ever need an LL Bean Pathfinder LED cap for? We never camp and rarely
work on things outside after dark. And then one night Eli squeezed his thin mischievous ass through a hole in the back fence and panicking we could not locate one of the numerous flashlights stashed about the house and then Agnes said the LL Bean Pathfinder LED cap that Norm gave me might work and sure enough LL Bean Pathfinder LED cap proved instrumental in locating the wayward lad now pinched and growing worried between the wooden fence and the old rusting metal hulk that the fence installers left in place instead of removing like they were supposed to do.

5.
I still have a claims tool kit replete with fine canvas tote bag in
the downstairs front closet. Norm assembled it and left it in my
care in case there were ever a time he needed to do a quick claims
inspection down here and had flown to the States on business that
lacked a tooling requirement. But it is no longer tool kit in a fine
canvas tote, but memento, wish, talisman, an in tact archaeology
trove and trigger for the way back machine and where I will always find:
a Stanley graphite shaft hammer,
a Big Johnson tape measure, secured before the branding demise,
FatMax utility knife,
Marples flush cut saw,
Empire mini level in neon green,
Tuck tape,
Tyvek tape,

two small bundles stainless steel siding nails bound with rubber bands,
one roll braided string neon green,
pair Husky flush cut nippers,
one Dasco Ultra Bar II,
one small Stanley pry bar,
Craftsmen utility mirror with telescoping handle, mirror secured with duct
tape because the damned mirror would always slide out of the tool,
a Vaughn Bear Claw pry bar a small square of purple felt rubber banded to
the sharp business end of the claw to protect reaching hands,
and sundry pieces of jobsite chaff: a piece of rotten wooden trim that clearly
illustrates that the original board had not been installed as per
manufacturer instruction, several bent siding nails waiting a frugal
straightening tap and re-use on another claim, bits of packaging from
the aforementioned list of tools.

OK, that is not exactly Carter's inventory of King Tutankhamun's tomb with
its giant statue of Anubis, 11 solar boat paddles or four gilded shrines, but
there again, what would I do with a statue of Anubis, 11 solar boat paddles or
four gilded shrines? One always finds occasional need for a hammer and
dammit I can never remember where I left mine last.

Chapter 82

Poem for the Koho Restaurant and Bar, YVR…

I hereby summon the muses, spirit bears, gods, Sasquatches, angels, nymphs, sprites, Thunderbirds and all other mystical beings of all the rivers, ocean and vast, verdant forests of the Pacific Northwest, wood basket of the world, that I might sing your praises, O mighty Koho Restaurant and Bar, International Terminal, Vancouver International Airport!

Mighty slaker of thirsts flown in from the distant East of Newark, New Jersey!

Purveyor of passable meat snacks! And a pretty decent Eggs Benedict!

Provider of almost comfortable chairs and stools!   Perfect for people watching
and the biding of time while waiting for my ride North or the arrival of another hale and hearty recruit for the long march to the distant, distal end of the Domestic Terminal!

Slinger of a consistent, well managed, buzz inducing flood of Kokanee, Glacier Fresh Beer, and Strongbow cider the year I stood stolid, determined watch until1PM local time, three long hours from my arrival at YVR, waiting for Craig and Norm. I am yet amazed that I left the premises under my own power and not as a passenger on one of the multitude of FREE exceptionally functional YVR luggage carts!

Take that Newark, JFK, Laguardia, Islip! FREE carts!

Into whose familiar, almost comfortable arms I collapsed the Sunday after Norm's service, waiting for my flight to distant Newark!

I must admit, these rank high among the saddest, loneliest hours in my life, but gentle reader that is the essence of an airport bar. Cheerleader in high times, provider of almost comfortable chairs and nearly quiet contemplation space during difficult ones.

And…Fuck these naysayers on Yelp, TripAdvisor and Urbanspoon!
What loser writes about an airport bar anyway? O wait…

Anyway, again I summon the muses, spirit bears, gods, Sasquatches, angels,
nymphs, sprites Thunderbirds and all other mystical critters of all the rivers,
ocean and vast forests of the Pacific Northwest, wood
basket of the world, that I might sing your praises, O mighty
Koho Restaurant and Bar!

The best joint in the entire…International Terminal at the Vancouver
International Airport!

Chapter 83

A generalissimo knows how to do things right…

I am sure that if you gentle reader or myself had a beautiful, cascading water feature constructed in our backyard replete with pond, babbling creek and a gentle falls we would throw a christening party replete with grilled succulent meats, sparkling wine, beer, Sangria, booze for the heavy hitters, hamburgers, hot dogs, cake for the kids and sweet toothed adults, etc & etc & etc.

I do not think any of us would consider let alone rig our truck bed water tight with tarps, pump it full of water, repair to one of the Asian fish markets to secure, after much negotiation, careful navigation of the obvious language barrier and provision of ample compensation for the breeching of the sale of live fish ordinance, six live trout.

And then transport said live trout carefully over the winding roadways of suburban
Vancouver, careful to not slosh all of the damned water out of the bed by stopping too damned fast at a light or taking a corner at too high of a speed thereby drawing attention to the fact that you have rigged your truck bed
water tight with tarps, pumped it full of water and are transporting six live trout in wanton defiance of the sale of live fish ordinance.

And finally release six live trout into the water feature such that that the kids at the party can toss a line and catch a fish and every one of the adult attendees and tangential friends informed of the event can one day say, You remember that time Norm put six live trout in the water feature? He was an absolute maniac. God I miss him. We all do.

Chapter 84

Balzams redux…

To steal a line of all of the gin joints in
the world there it is high on the third
shelf at Dark Horse Restaurant in down
town River City literally six blocks from
my house sitting by itself, likely to
keep it out of the way of the more
briskly rotating liquors in fact it
is displayed more as art than beverage
on offer, its distinctive opaque
black bottle with gold lettering
obscuring whether there is actually
booze in there at all. I have to ask the
bartender

Is there actually booze in
that bottle?

I'll have to check. In all of
my time here I have never
poured a drink from that
bottle.

There is a good reason for
that.

It's full. How do you take
it?

Let's try two neat.

Big mistake, we try to swirl and sniff
like it's cognac or a delicate aperitif
it smells like dirt there maybe
a hint of black licorice, maybe, maybe not
Agnes says generously,

It's definitely Earthy.

The first tentative swig produces a
similar result and Agnes pushes her

glass toward me

I would have to agree with
her assessment, but I have
made the commitment and cannot
shirk it, so I choke back my glass
and convince our benefactor for
the evening that he should partake
for the liquor's obvious curative
powers.

It is not that some drinks are not to
be drunk, some drinks should be
drunk solely as shooters where pain
is minimized, fleeting and your
tongue never quite has the time to
tell your brain you idiot this tastes
like shit before the demon distillate
hits your gut and no matter how much
character it has booze can never
replace the man.

I am NOT drinking that. It's
disgusting.

If it tastes that bad, it has to cure
something.

Chapter 85

A note on tragedy…

I came across some wise words while
watching television (an oxymoron for
certain,) the 9th Earl Spencer shared this
observation about the sudden
loss of his sister 20 years ago

The pain is the same,
there are fewer tears.

So we have that slice of
icy comfort going for us.

Chapter 86

Before leaving to use the washroom of the Quick
Stop just off

Exit 5
Front Street
Binghamton

of Interstate 81, Agnes reminds me, "Slavik up the car while I run in ok?"

"On it!"

So before topping off the tank I take the bag of trip detritus: empty beef jerky
bags, egg McMuffin wrappers, candy wrappers, water bottles, energy
drink cans (road trips are an excuse to fiendishly consume junk food all
sorts) hanging from the stick shift, ease its contents into the public
trash can next to the gas pump and re-hang the empty
bag on the shifter.

Norm showed me that life hack years back. Dropping an immense bag of
claim remnants policed up from the rear of the rented SUV: shards of rotted
wood, bent nails beyond a salvaging tap, empty water bottles, granola bar
wrappers, spent Starbucks cups, Tyvek tape that had doubled back on itself
and could
not be separated (shit is STICKY brother) and dropped it in the public
trash can outside of the Panera Bread in Hampton Bays.

And sure it seems a small thing, but it is an immense relief not to have to
clean up
an accumulated pile of shit in addition to unpacking the car after you have
driven
the nine to ten hours necessary to complete a trip from Riverhead, New York
to
Stoney Creek, Ontario.

And besides, it is why my car stays generally clean because the bag now
hangs continually from the stick shift and the everyday trash has a home
rather than annoyingly rolling around my peripheral vision on the passenger
side floorboards or worse wending its way under my feet while I drive.

Safety generated by improved organizational efforts, perfectly Norm.

Nay saying conscience:
Of course, there are bigger life improvements in the offing if you really wanted to pay attention, like following Norm's lead, not fiendishly consume junk food when traveling and make better food choices in general.

You would cut down the last Joy Tree in the rainforest if you could.

It is what I do.

Afterward

The Punch List...

And so we are down to gritty brass gentle reader, our
Punch List down to three items. I still need pieces: about
the first time I had occasion to meet Norm, the Cowboy
Junkies concert at the Mary Seaton Room, Kleinhans
Music Hall, Buffalo, NY and I wanted to do something
about Norm's dedication to the BC Lions of the Canadian
Football League. After that, I think the book is complete,
more or less (or will it be ever?) But as anyone who has built a
house knows the last things on the Punch List are the most difficult to
cross off the Punch List and it is hard to stay focused on the
tasks at hand and not float toward visions of new houses,
new projects, new views and sure this effort goes far beyond
the completion of a house and is much more psychologically
fraught, but it is here where we separate the builders from
the former landscapers who are woefully overmatched and where
this project could become just another one of my incomplete
masterpieces: the renovation of the back porch, the nearly finished
rear half of the kitchen, the 50% re-sided exterior of the house and
even this little poem is diversion, like being asked to add an
outdoor shower a week before the project closes when we
really should be focused on the three tasks at hand and so
I ask that the Gods of Coastal British Columbia and Jesus
(if He's at all interested) to bring, whisper, chant, scream these
three songs so we can all start building the next house.

Amen.

ABOUT THE AUTHOR

Steven Kramer

Steven Kramer is an internationally adored author, poet, and amateur chef. He has authored a poetry collection called East Main. He performs his work in many an open mic and is a member of Poetry Street. He is also a political activist for common sense and leaders who actually give a fuck about the little people. Steven lives in Long Island with an elderly yet feisty dog and a kindle of kittens that moved into his house after a short stint in his collapsing garage-slash-feral cat condominium.

CONNECT WITH THE AUTHOR

Steven Kramer

themindattic.com

facebook.com/themindattic

twitter.com/themindattic

Made in the USA
Columbia, SC
10 August 2023

5fee6ff5-9f12-4ef2-a2d9-8174f35188a8R01